NewMusicShelf

Anthology of New Music
Mezzo-Soprano, Vol. 1

Curated by Megan Ihnen

Foreword by Libby Larsen

NewMusicShelf
www.newmusicshelf.com

NEWMUSICSHELF, INC.

Published in the United States of America
by NewMusicShelf, Inc.
34-29 32nd St., 3rd floor, Astoria, NY 11106
www.newmusicshelf.com

Copyright © 2018 by NewMusicShelf, Inc.

First printing 2018

All rights reserved. No part of this publication may be reproduced,
stored in a retrieval system, or transmitted in any form or by any
means, electronic, mechanical, photocopying, recording, or otherwise,
without the prior permission of the publisher.

This anthology is dedicated to Phyllis, David, and all educators who encourage their students to explore the unknown.

Contents

Acknowledgments vii
Foreword by Libby Larsen ix
Editor's Preface x
Introduction xi

Michael Betteridge: First time he kissed me... (2013) 1

Mark Buller: From the Unreal (2017) 7
    from To the Soul

Stephen DeCesare: Sister Maude (2015) 9

Douglas Fisk: love is a place (2003) 17
    from Three Songs

Matt Frey: Without a Thorn (2017) 21

Jodi Goble: I Would Live In Your Love (2013) 27
    from Three Teasdale Songs

Ricky Ian Gordon: Let Evening Come (2000) 33
    from Late Afternoon

Cara Haxo: Im Harren (2016) 41

Cameron Lam: Death (2013) 45
    from Fragments of Solitude

Cecilia Livingston: Give Me Your Hand (2015) 52

Shona Mackay: Silent Noon (2016) 62
    from Three Songs

Tony Manfredonia: Prairie Dawn (2017) 67

Nicole Murphy: air stirs (2015) 70

Eric Pazdziora: Thief's Song (2013) 72
    from The Accidental Feast of the Holy Fool

Frances Pollock: Scheherezade (2017) 81

Julia Seeholzer: Prayer at my parting (2016) 86
    from Portraits of Disquiet

Alan Theisen: Look Down Fair Moon (2017) 93

Dennis Tobenski: Good Bones (2017) 96

Moe Touizrar: Dark Pines Under Water (2003) 105

Ed Windels: Blackbird Etude (2013) 120
    from Opus 22 Songs

About the Curator 129
About the Composers 130
Supplemental Materials 150

Foreword

Congratulations! You hold in your hands the *NewMusicShelf Anthologies of New Music*, a four-volume, curated treasure trove of 80 songs penned by your colleague composers and composed for you, singer of songs, teller of tales, bearer of our zeitgeist. Discover and prize these songs. They are yours now, in your keeping, waiting to rise on your breath and sing through your voices.

You might think of these four volumes of song as living-history - a vibrant mix of singers, collaborative instrumentalists, composers and our audiences. A wide range of the many excellent composers writing art song today are represented here. They are a community of composers who love the human voice and devote their talent and time to composing new work for it. We honor these composers through performance, of course, by singing the songs they write for us. We also must remind ourselves that we need to honor their work by respecting their need to support themselves with compensation in the form of the royalties they collect from sales of their music. We urge you to support your composers by resisting the temptation to photocopy and distribute music from these song collections. As the world becomes more and more digital, we think it essential that these collections of songs are available only in print. In the years to come we will be delighted to discover the *NewMusicShelf Anthologies of New Music* on pianos, bookshelves and music stands, but even more delighted to hear you filling the air with the sound of your singing - these songs - everywhere!

— Libby Larsen

Acknowledgments

I would like to personally thank Dennis Tobenski for the opportunity to curate such a volume as well as my fellow curators including Dennis, Laura trickling, and Michael Kelly. I would also like to acknowledge Phyllis Bryn-Julson and David Smooke. Without their mentorship, I would not have discovered this deep and abiding passion for new music.

— Megan Ihnen

Editor's Preface

This volume - and series of publications - exists to introduce performing musicians to the amazing variety of composers living and writing today. Whether you're a student, teacher, or professional, this collection was created with you in mind.

Every song is appropriate for a professional or student recital, and many songs were selected for their didactic possibilities: shifting meters, asymmetrical rhythms, various degrees of difficulty with pitch materials or non-traditional performance techniques, etc.

Across all four inaugural volumes of these anthologies, the primary criterion has been the curator's willingness to stand behind their selections: to be willing to perform and record every song, and make their selections without reservation. These are songs that singers should *know*, and should perform. These are composers that singers should *know*, and should work with.

And *you* are performers that composers should get to know and work with! We are all a part of a community that makes music, and we can only be better and stronger together.

As the creator of this series, I've had to personally define my short-, medium-, and long-term goals for the project. My short-term goal is simple: you getting to know these songs, and performing them. I stand behind every song and every composer, and hope that you find your own connection to these songs.

My medium-term goal is linked to a minor feature of these volumes: notice that underneath many of the song titles there is a bit of text: "from _____". Many of these songs are from song cycles or song sets. I encourage you to check out those cycles, as well as the composer's other vocal works! My medium-term goal? That you and your colleagues get to know more of the works by these composers than are represented here. This is a mere sliver of these composers' output, and their catalogs are worth exploring!

My long-term goal? Let's just say that I have plans....

I encourage you to look beyond the borders of the voice-type specific nature of these volumes. Many of these songs were written without gender or voice type in mind, and so are worth exploring by every singer.

— Dennis Tobenski
Founder of NewMusicShelf

INTRODUCTION

It was an honor and a pleasure to be asked to curate volume 1 of the NewMusicShelf Anthology of New Music for Mezzo-Soprano. As a tireless advocate of contemporary classical music for the voice, this anthology is an important way for me to highlight the high-quality work of composers of our time. My curation process took into account the calibre and merits of the score, the musical sounds, and the text. Plus, I dedicated my selections to providing a range for different ability levels and technical objectives. My thoughts took into account my own desires in art song as well as the desires of my students and audiences across different locations. It is my sincere hope that you will find something you love to sing, teach, or present in this anthology.

— Megan Ihnen

First time he kissed me...

E.B. BROWNING

MICHAEL BETTERIDGE
(2012)

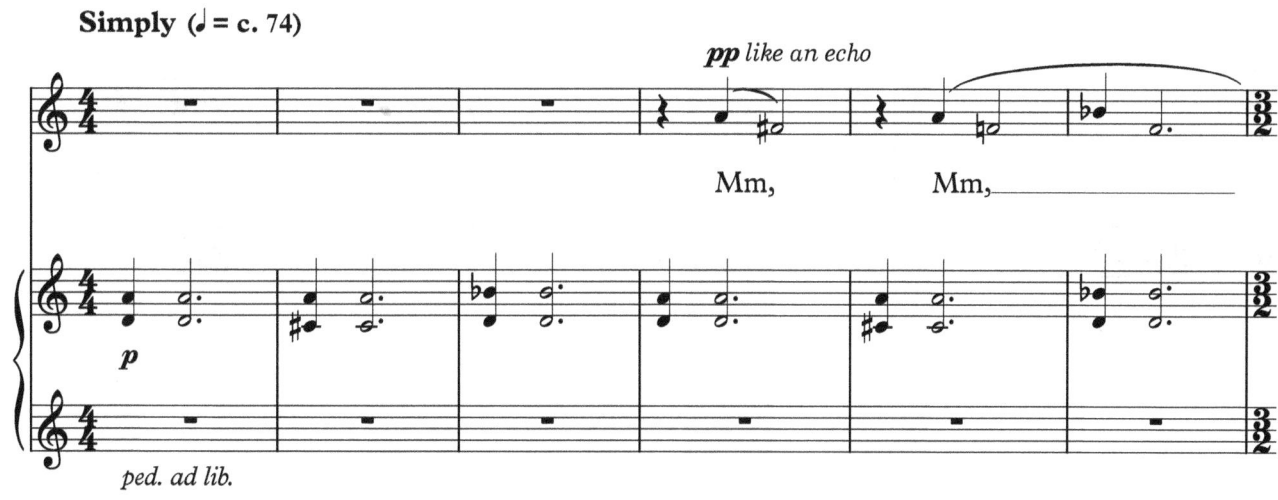

Copyright © 2012 by Michael Betteridge

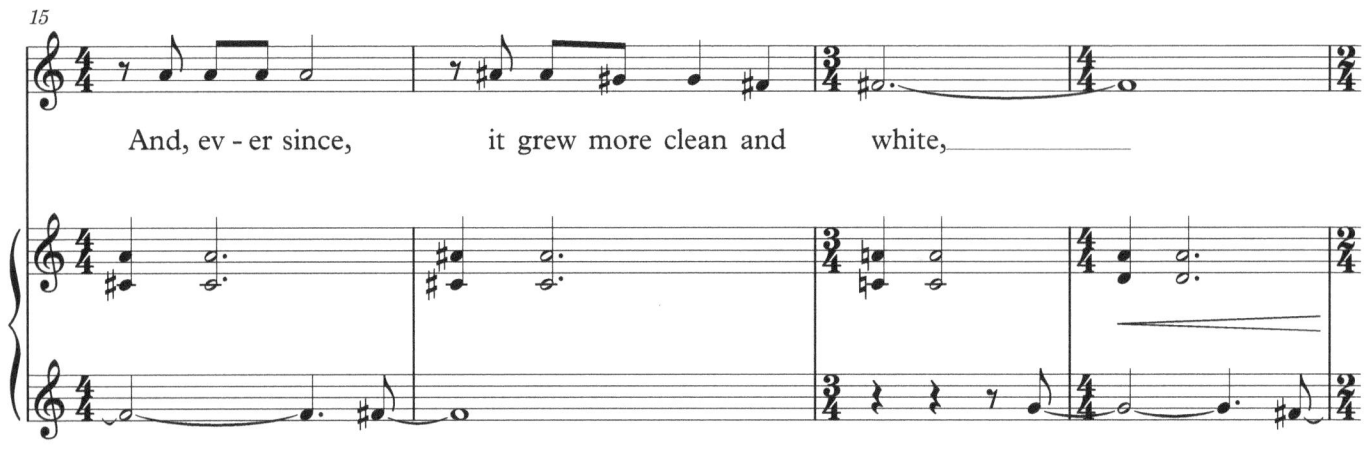

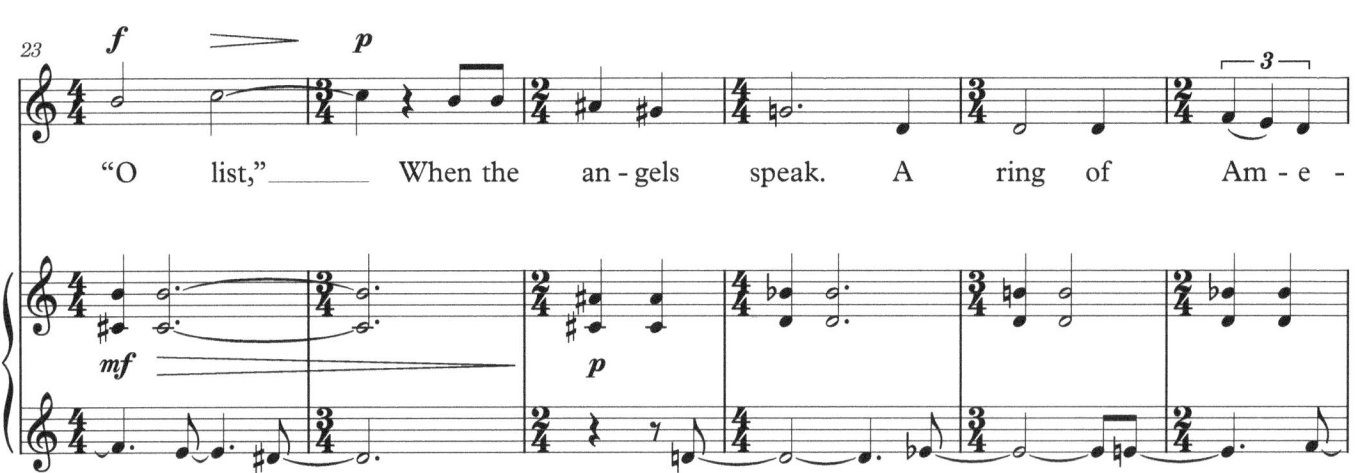

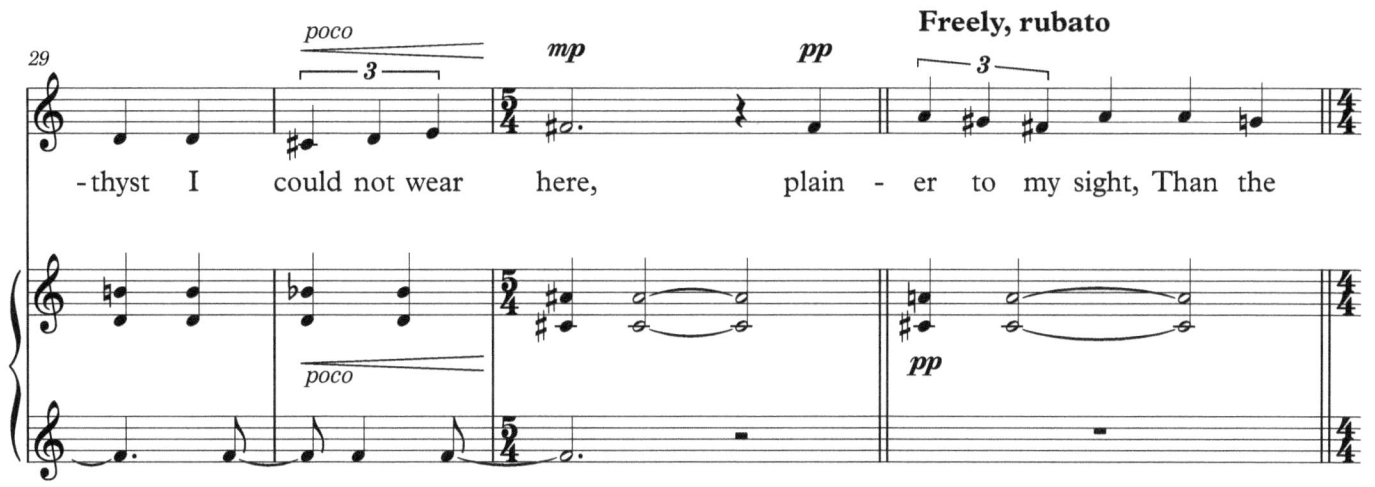

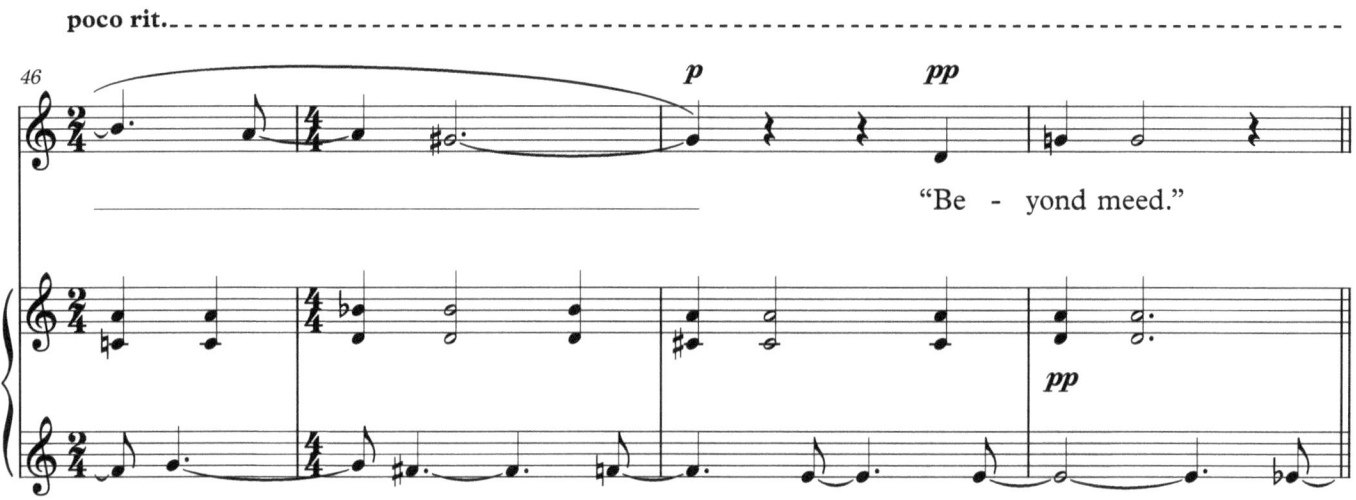
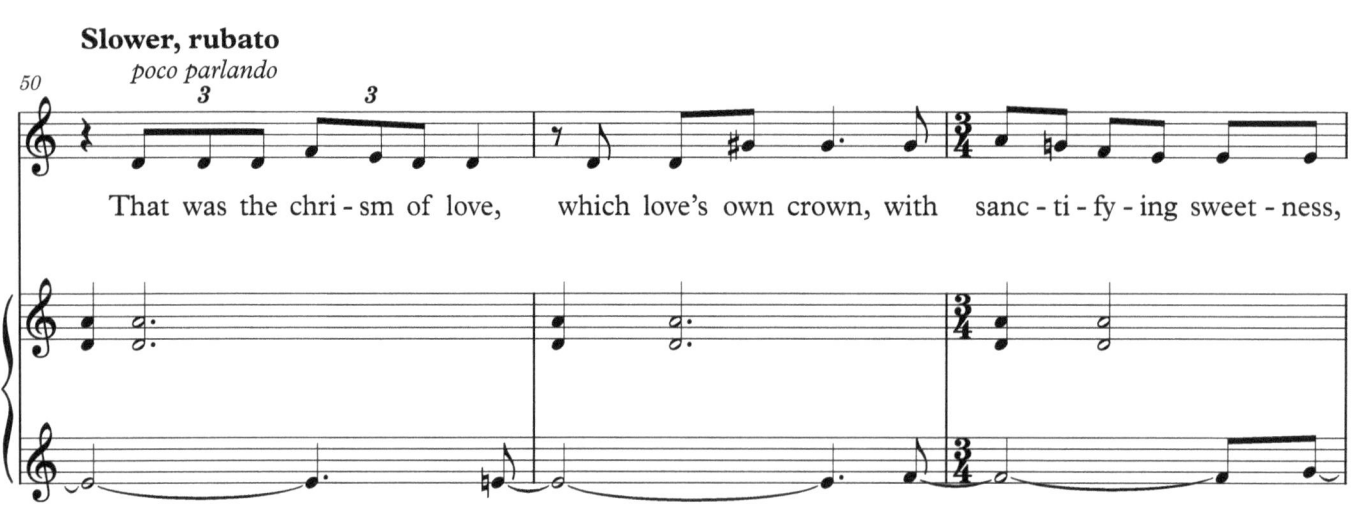

From the Unreal
from *To the Soul*

from The Upanishads

MARK BULLER
(2017)

Semplice (♩ = 76)

From the un-real lead me to the real.

From darkness lead me to light.

Copyright © 2017 Mark Buller (ASCAP). All Rights Reserved.

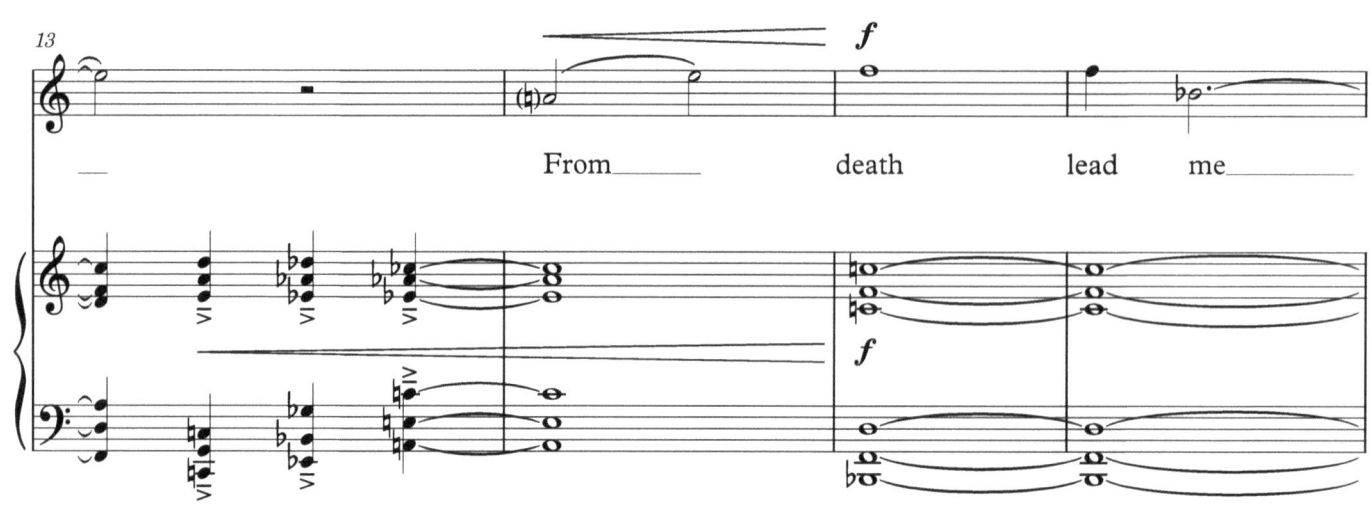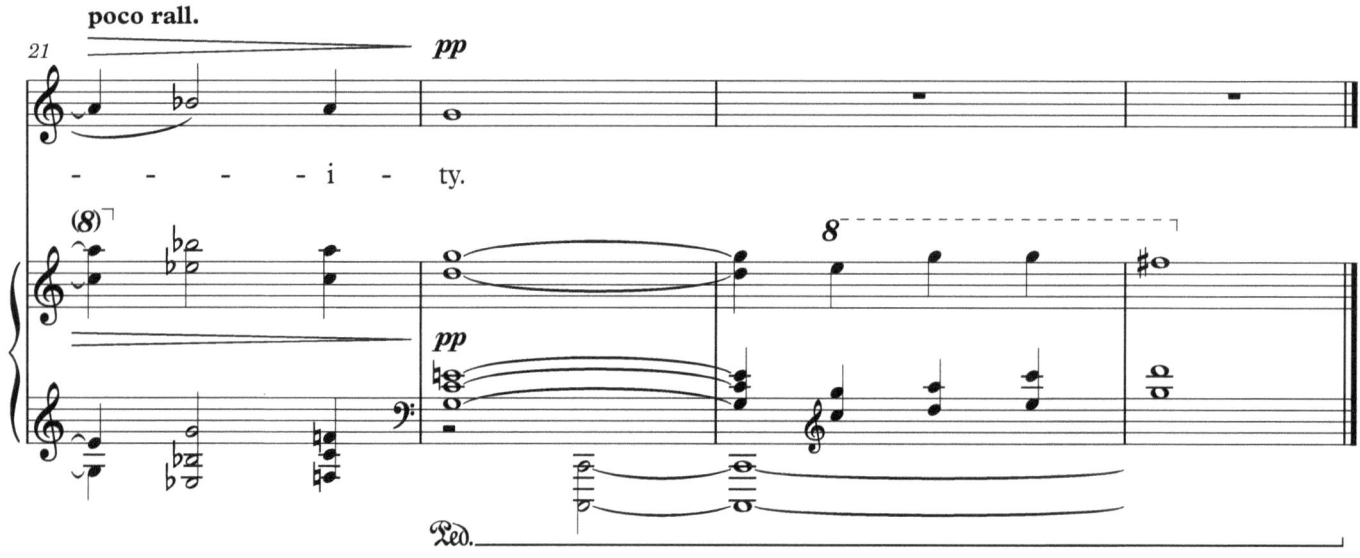

for Katie Miller
Sister Maude

CHRISTINA ROSSETTI

STEPHEN DECESARE
(2015)

Bluesy, 'gut-bucket' style (♩ = 100)

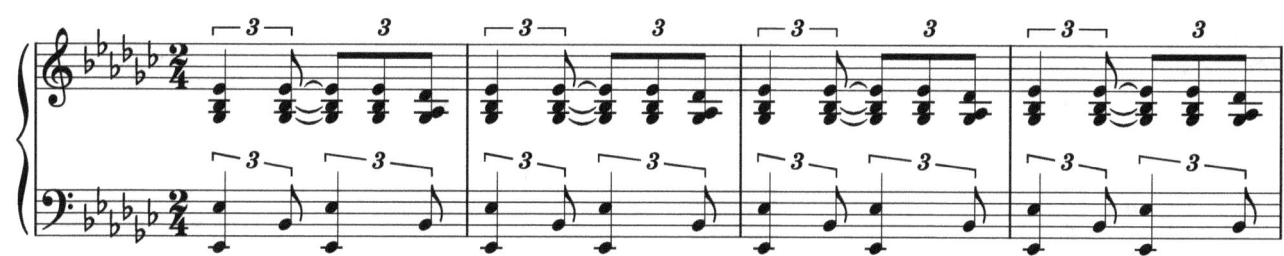

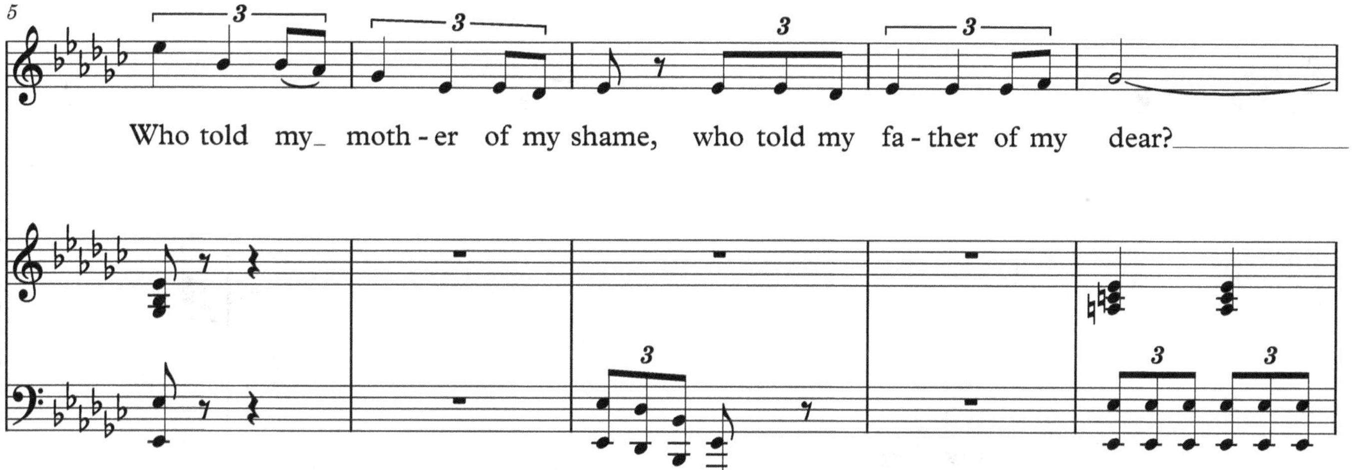

Who told my mother of my shame, who told my father of my dear?

Oh who but Maude, my sister Maude, who lurked to spy and

Copyright © 2015 exsultetmusic.com. All Rights Reserved.

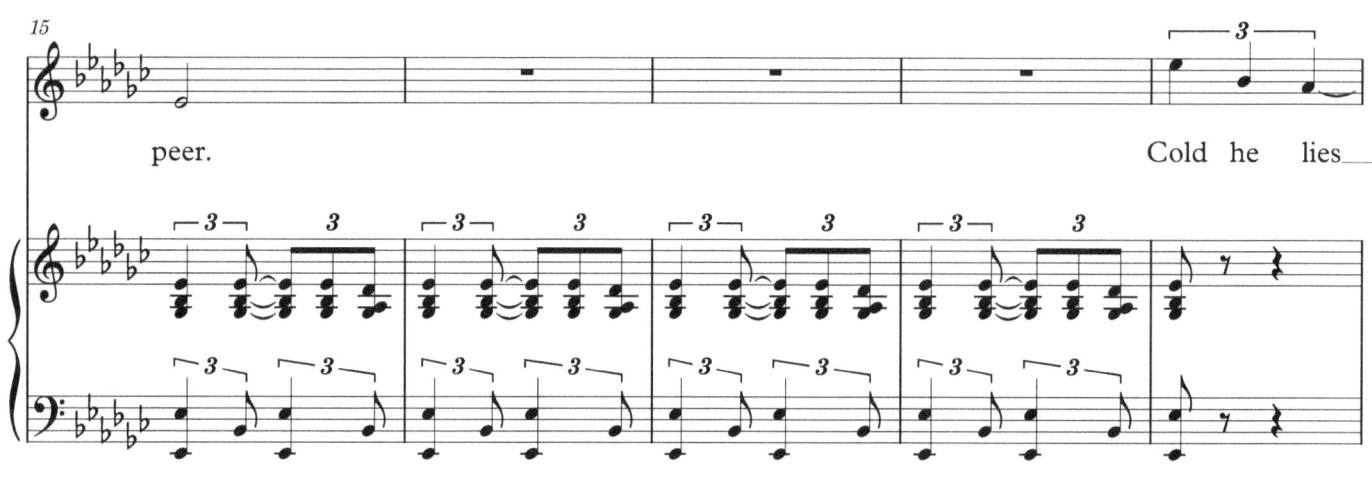

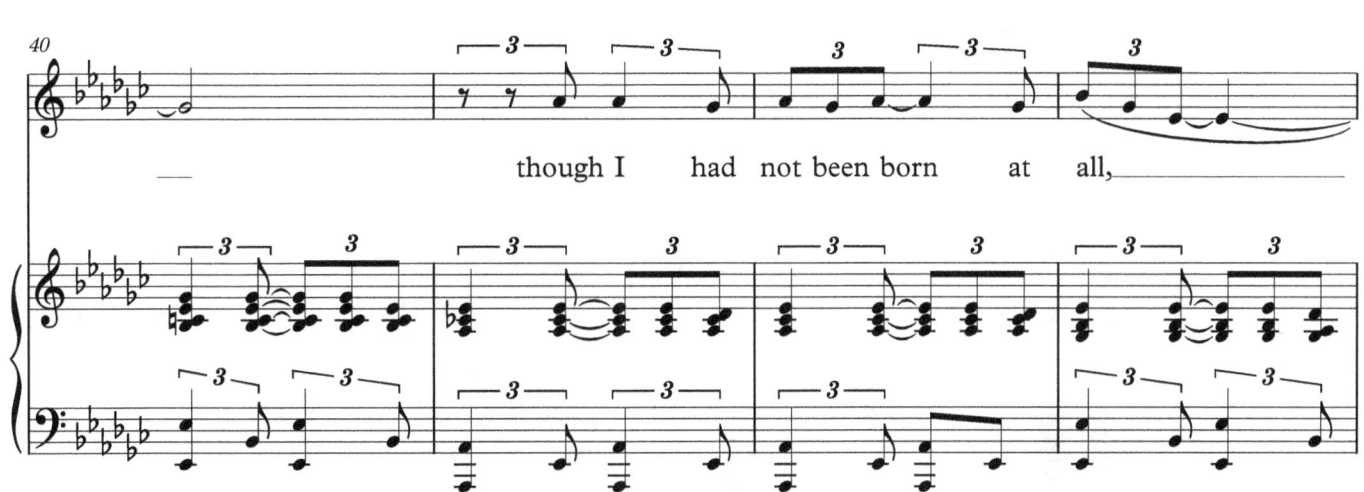

14

shall get no sleep ei-ther ear-ly or late.

My fa-ther may wear a gold-en gown, my

moth-er a crown may win; If my dear and I knocked on Heav-en-

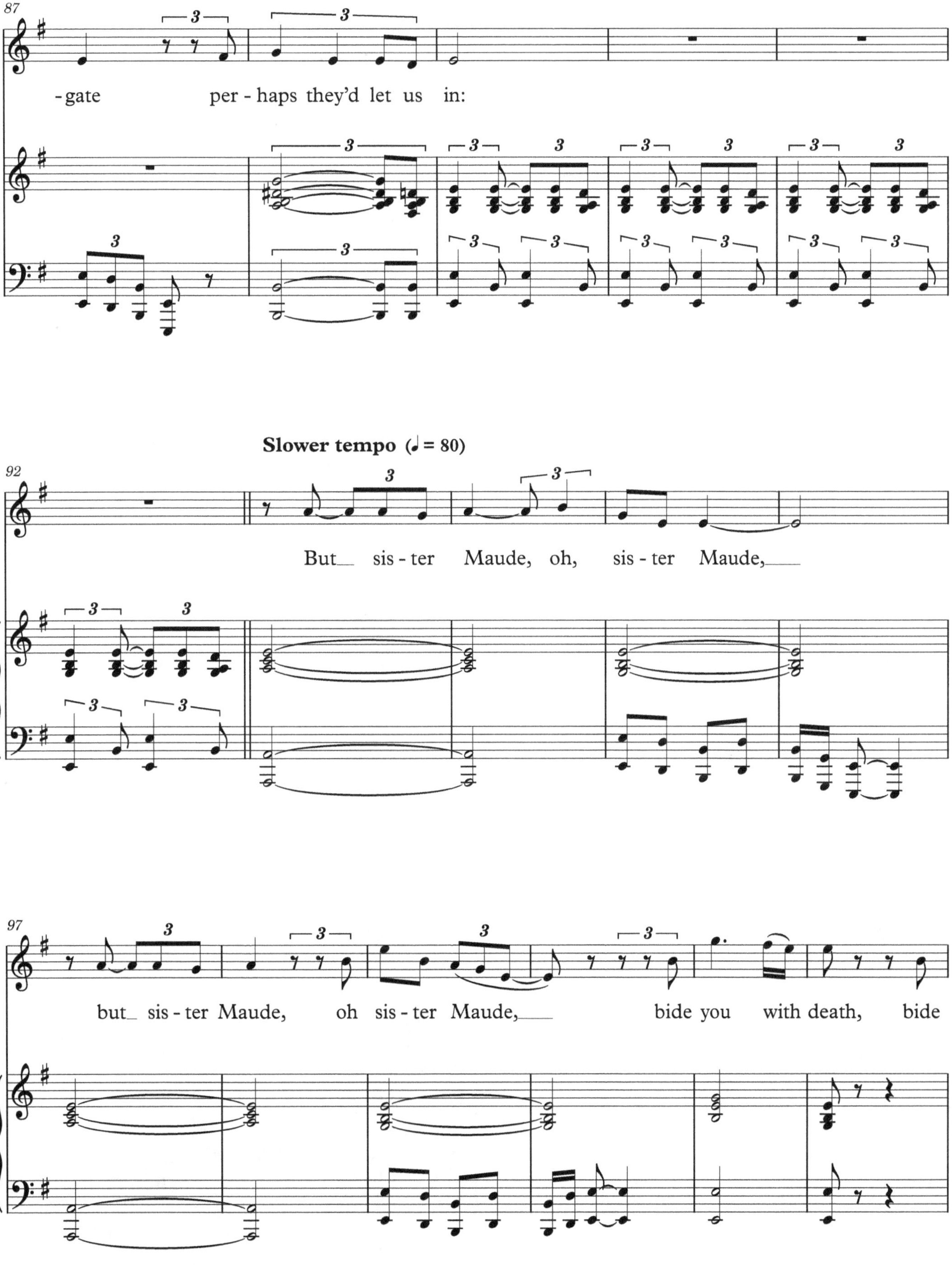
87
-gate per - haps they'd let us in:
Slower tempo (♩ = 80)
92
But_ sis - ter Maude, oh, sis - ter Maude,___
97
but_ sis - ter Maude, oh sis - ter Maude,___ bide you with death, bide

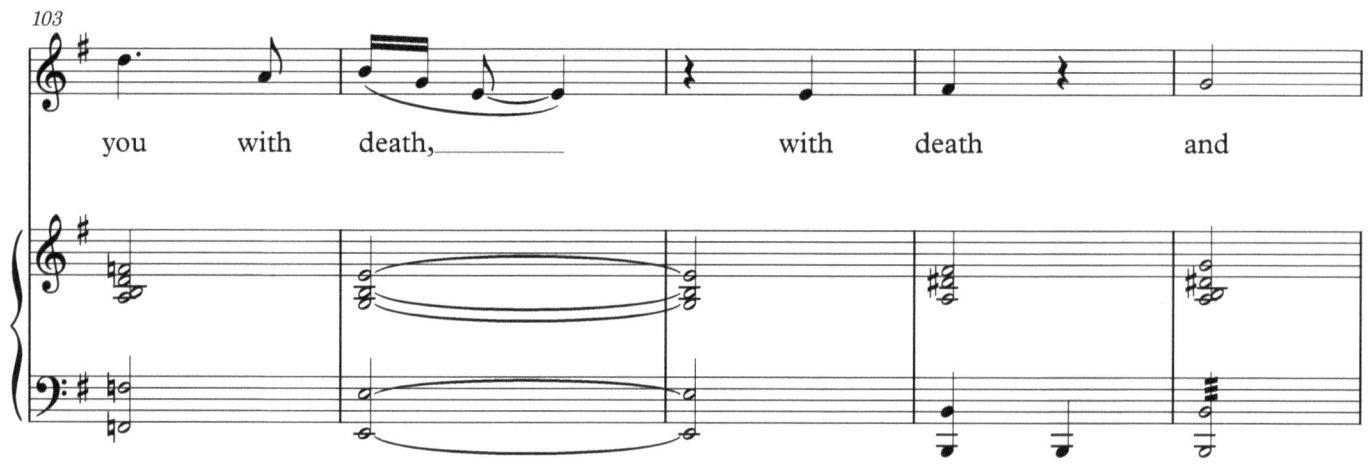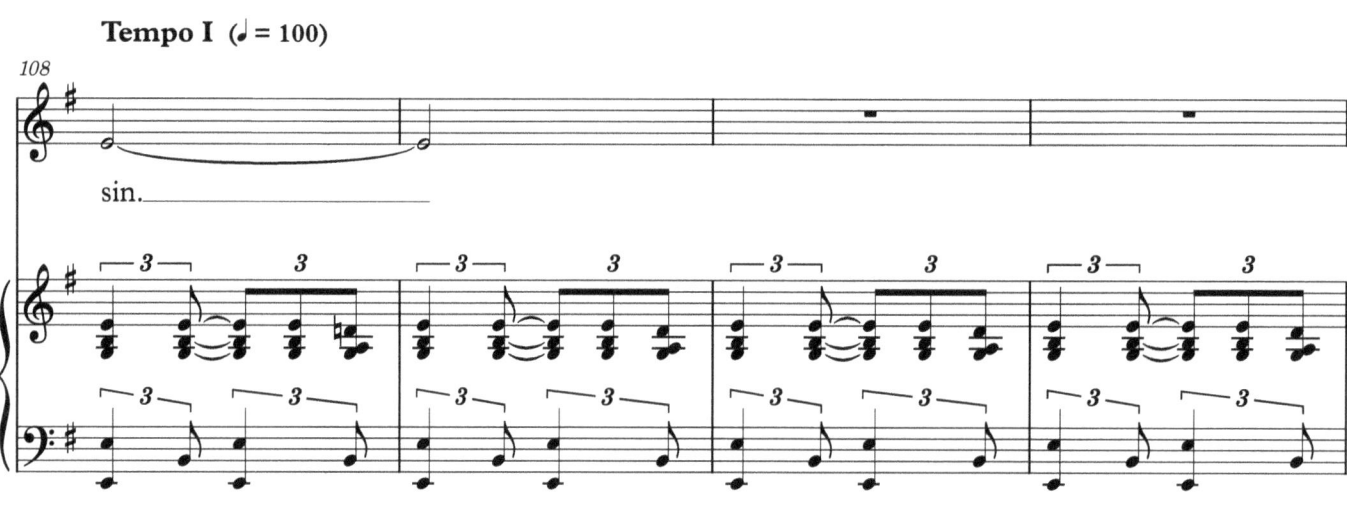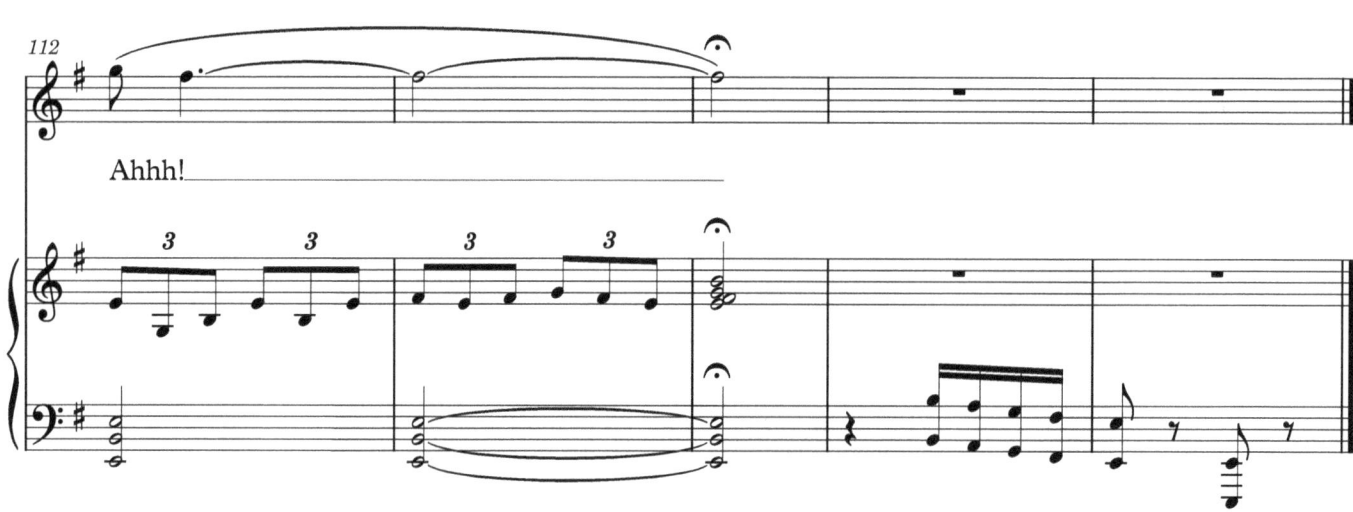

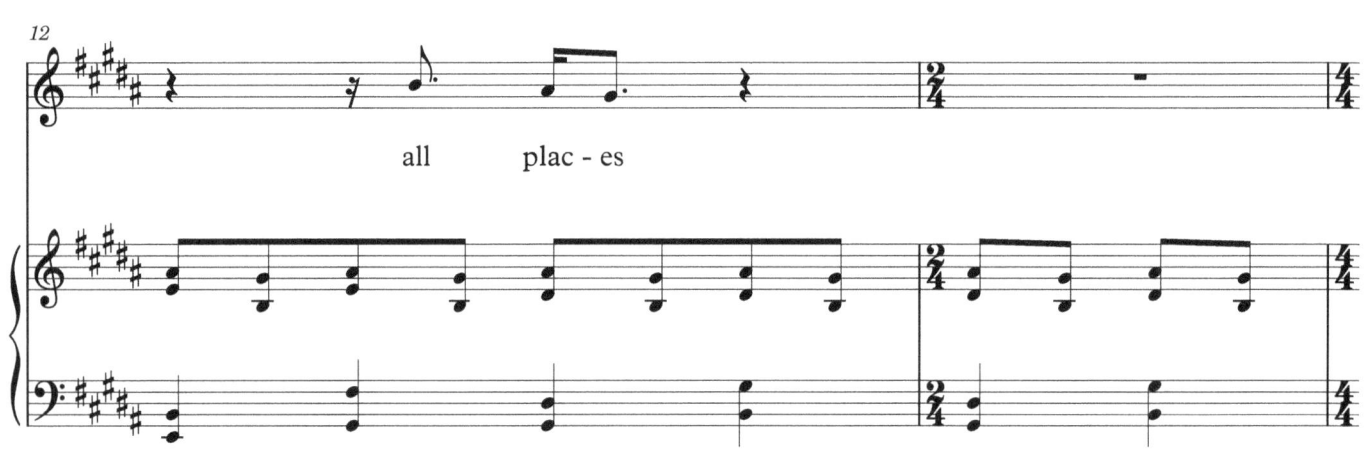

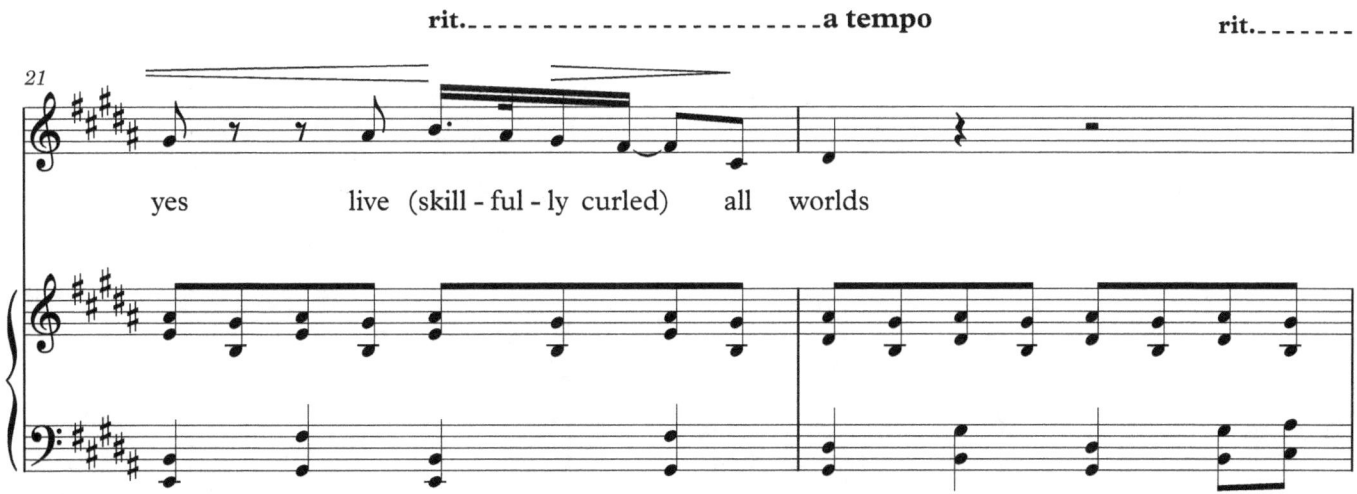

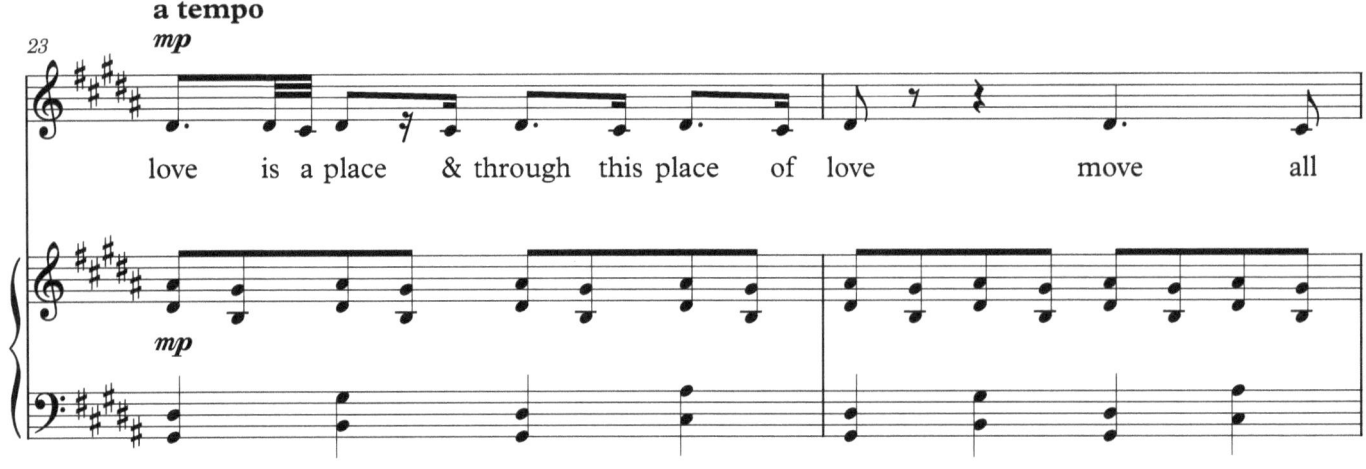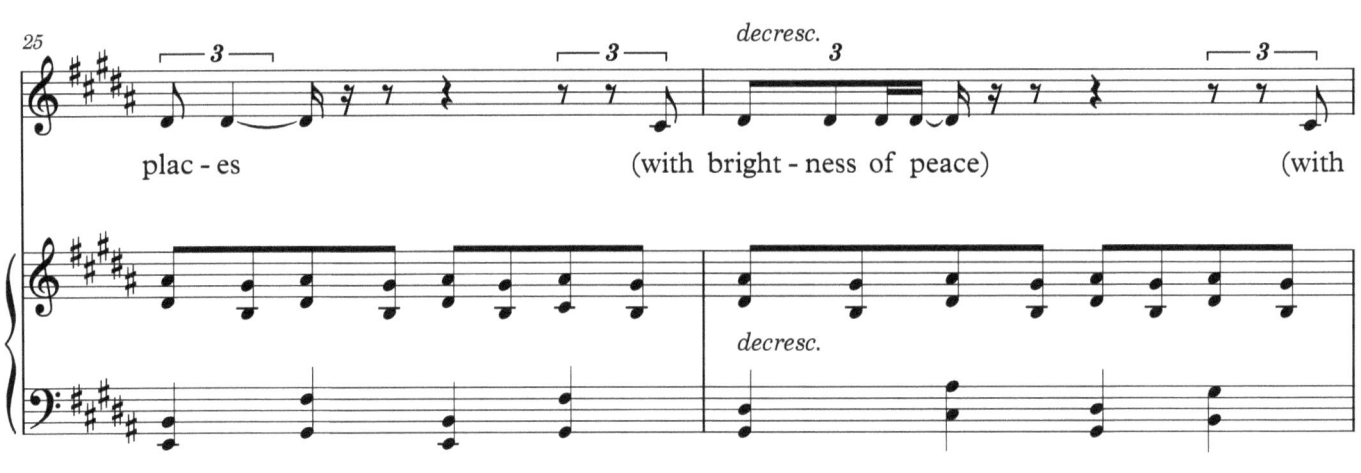

for Jen Anaya
Without A Thorn

Text and Music:
MATT FREY
(2017)

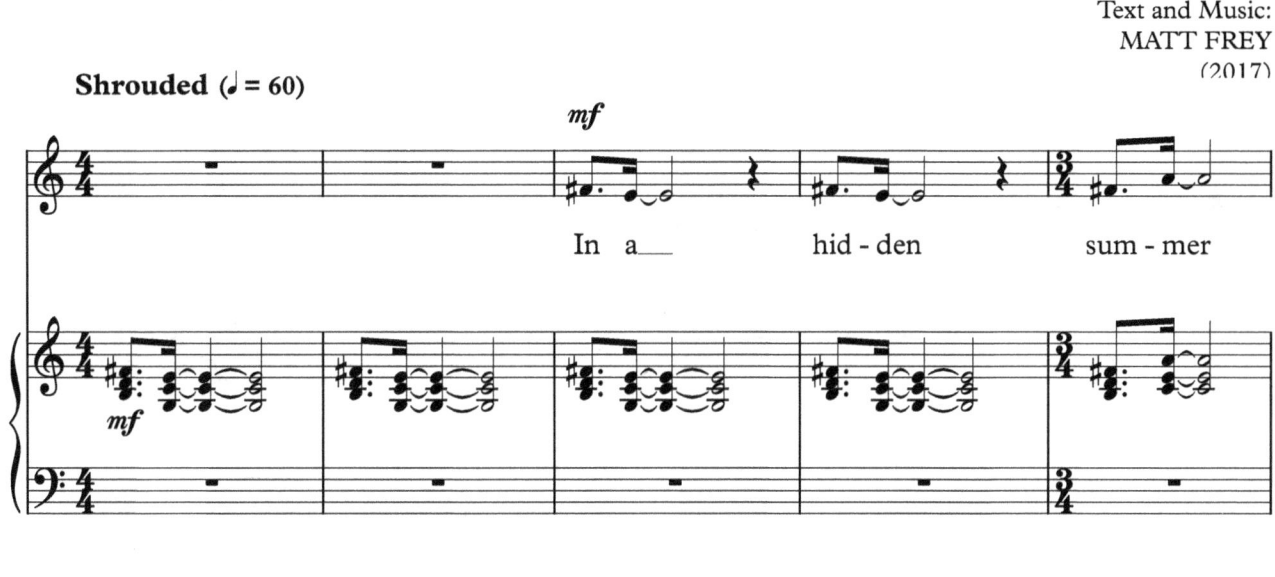

Copyright © 2017 by Matt Frey.

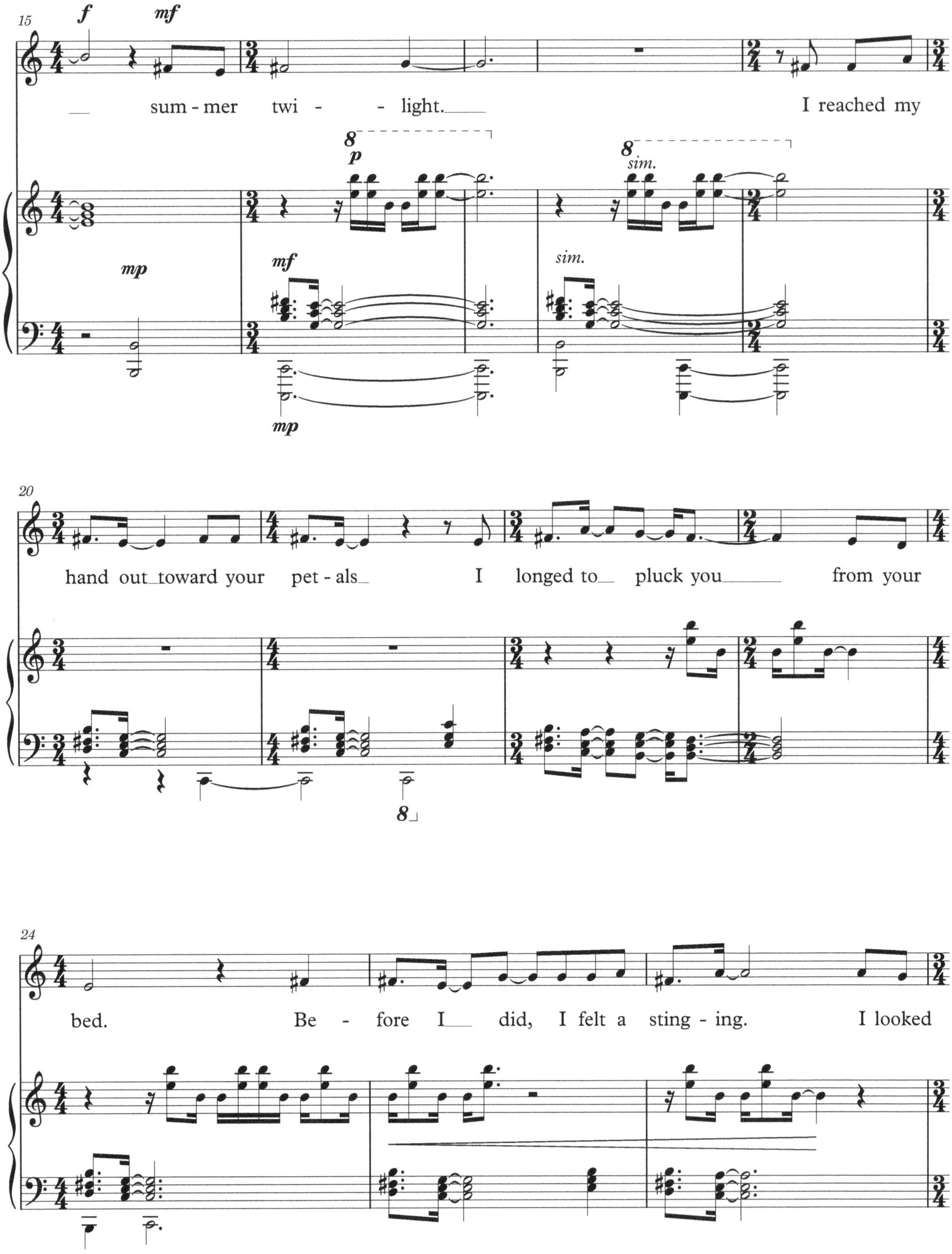

Jointly commissioned by the Music Teachers National Association and the Iowa Music Teachers Association

I Would Live In Your Love
from *Three Teasdale Songs*

SARA TEASDALE

JODI GOBLE
(2013)

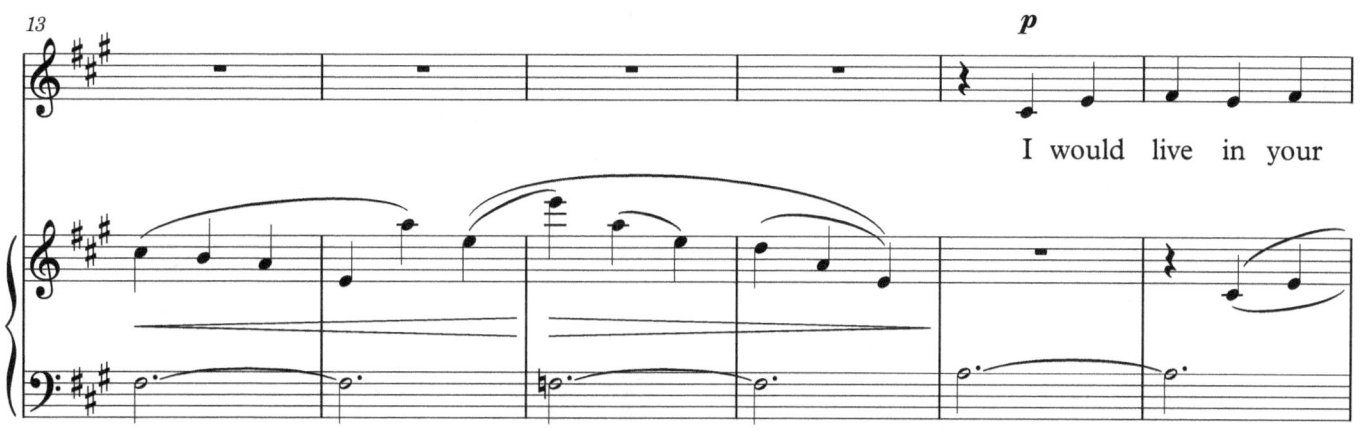

Copyright © 2013 Three Teasdale Songs by Jodi Goble.
All Rights Reserved.

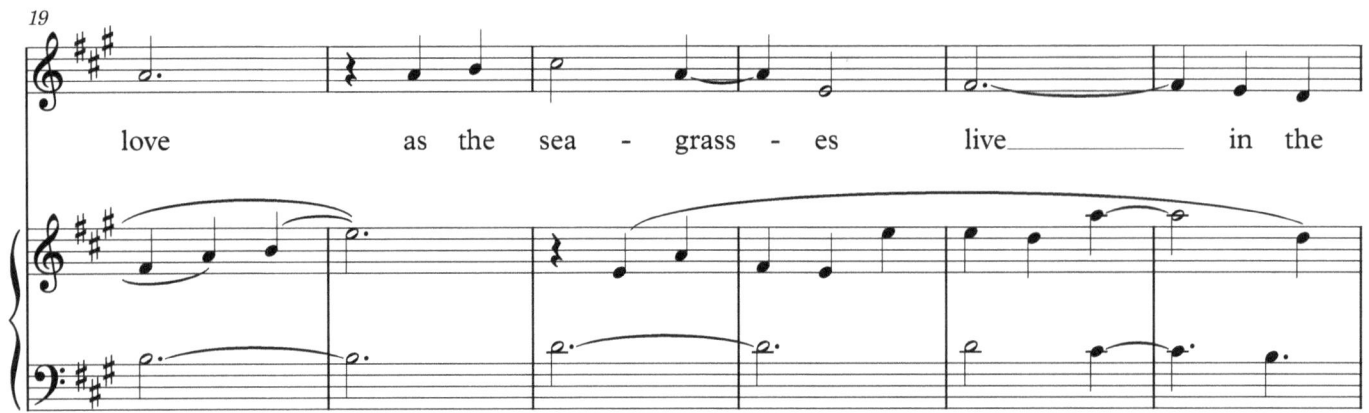

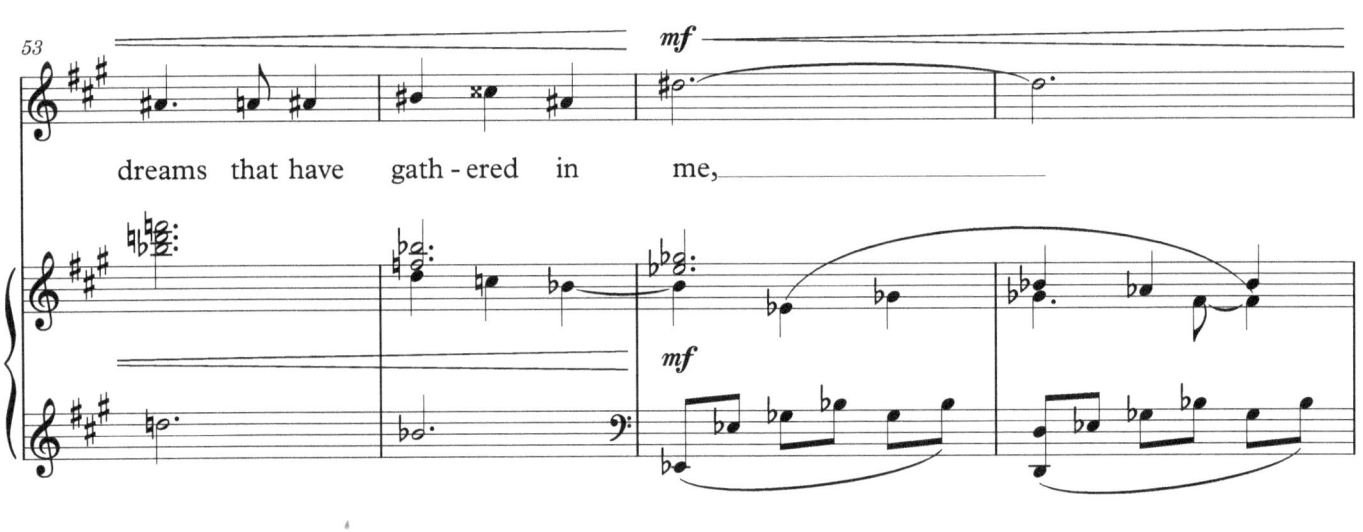

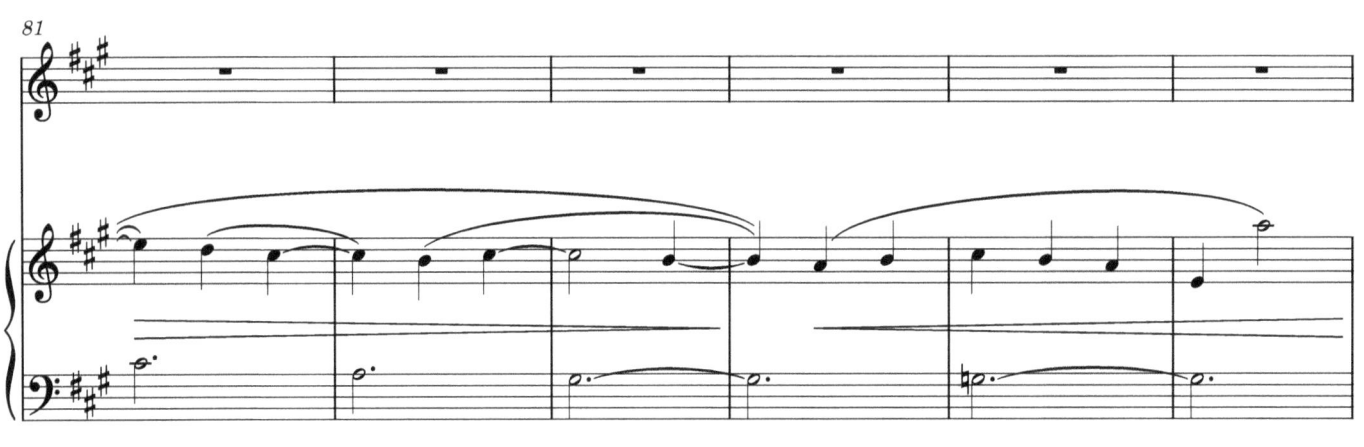
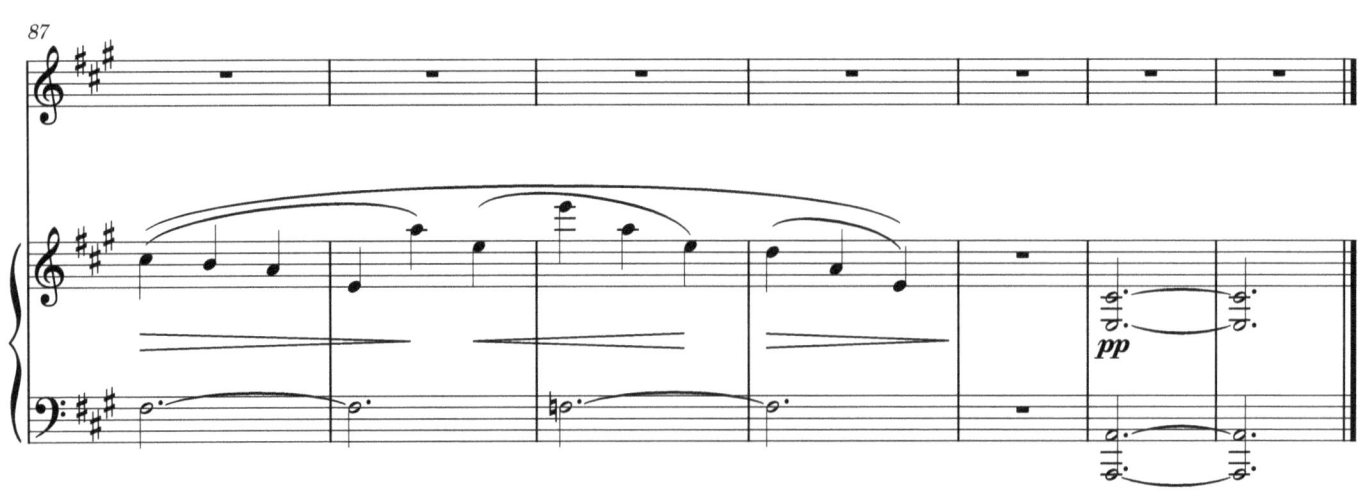

for my sister, Susan Gordon Lydon
Let Evening Come
from *Late Afternoon*

JANE KENYON RICKY IAN GORDON

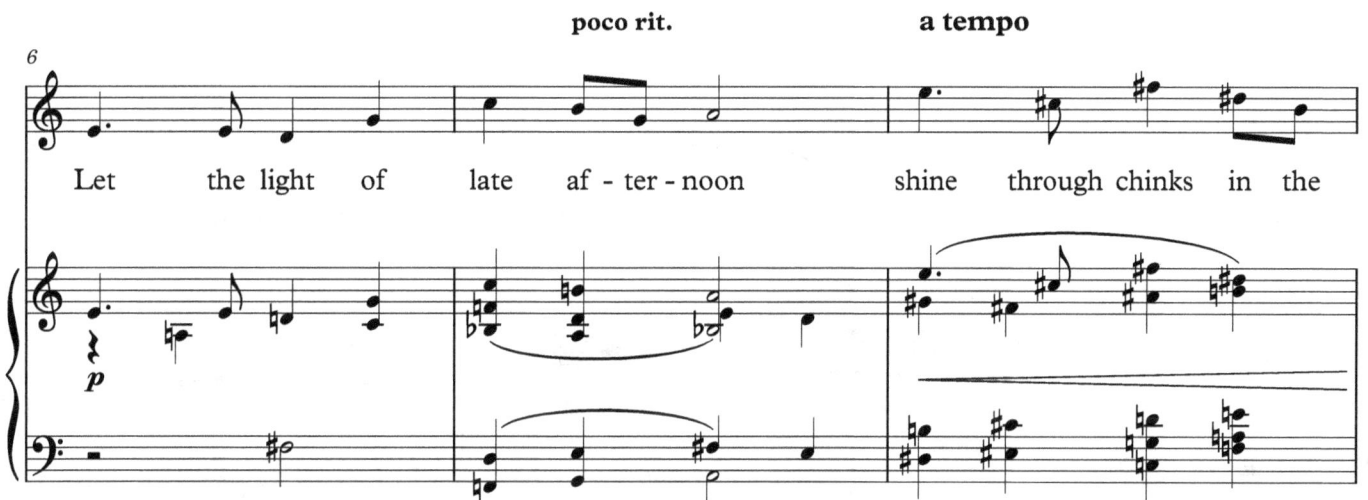

Let the light of late af-ter-noon shine through chinks in the

barn, mov-ing up the bales as the sun moves

Music Copyright © 2007 by Carl Fischer LLC
International Copyright Secured.
All rights reserved, including performance rights.

34

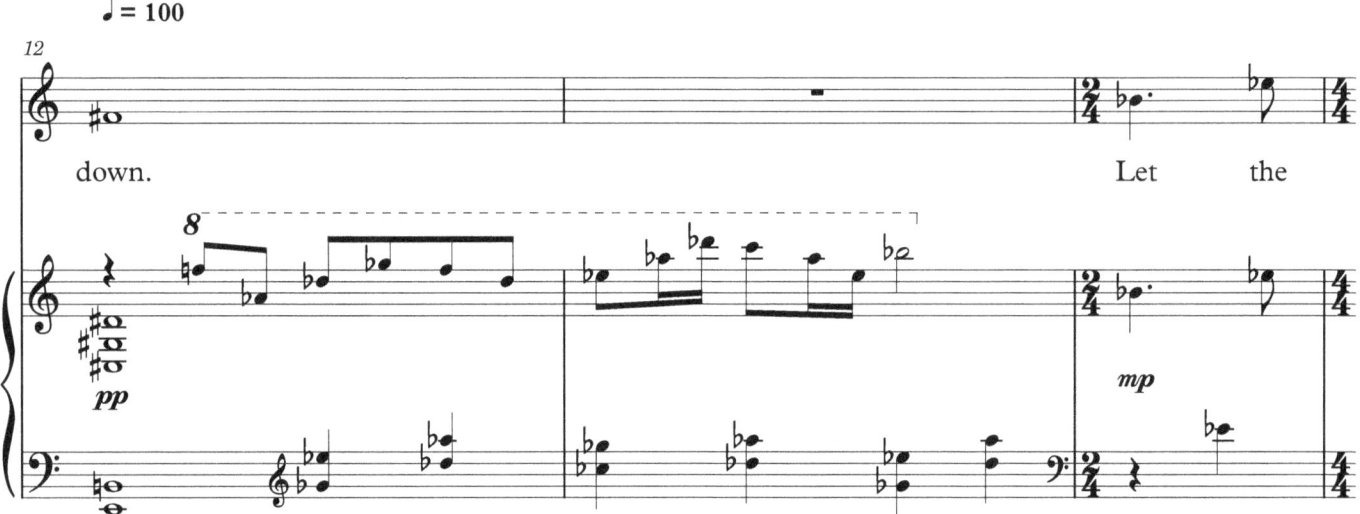

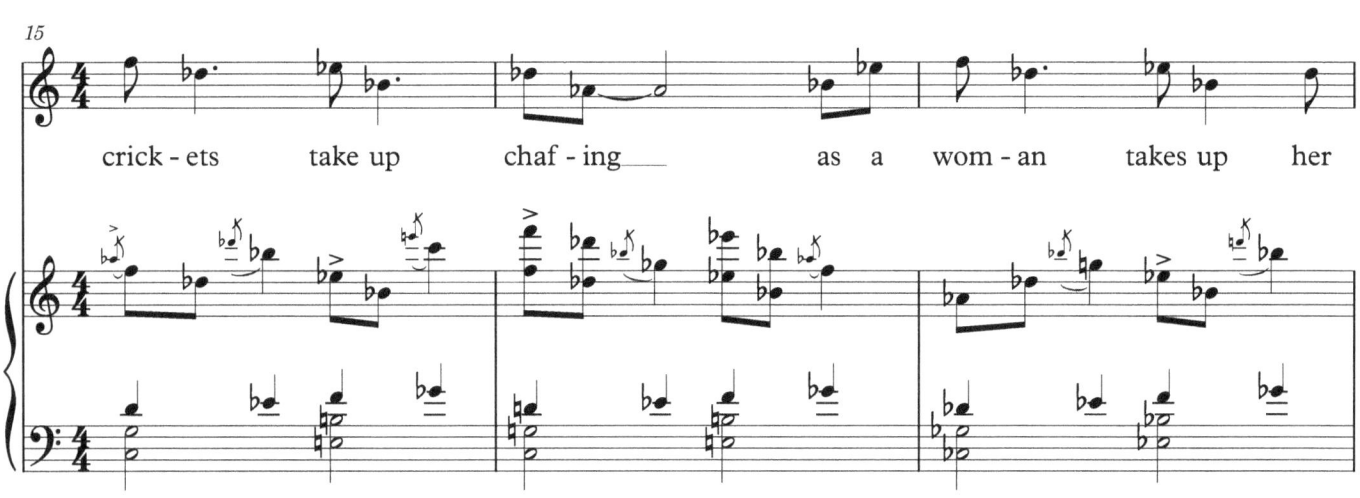

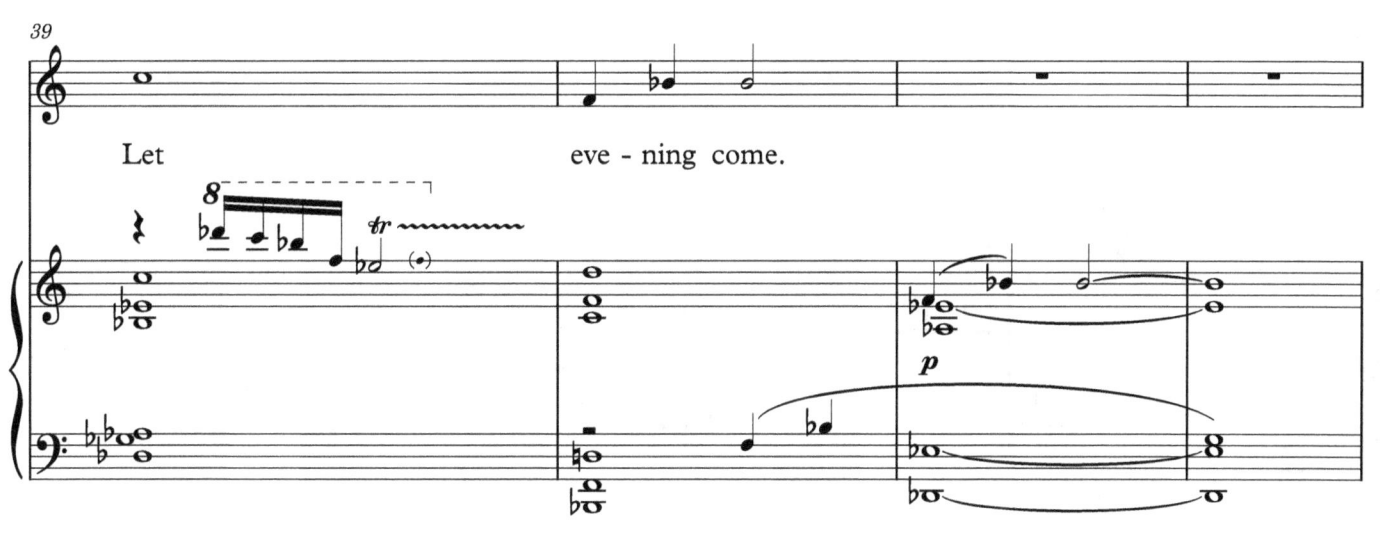

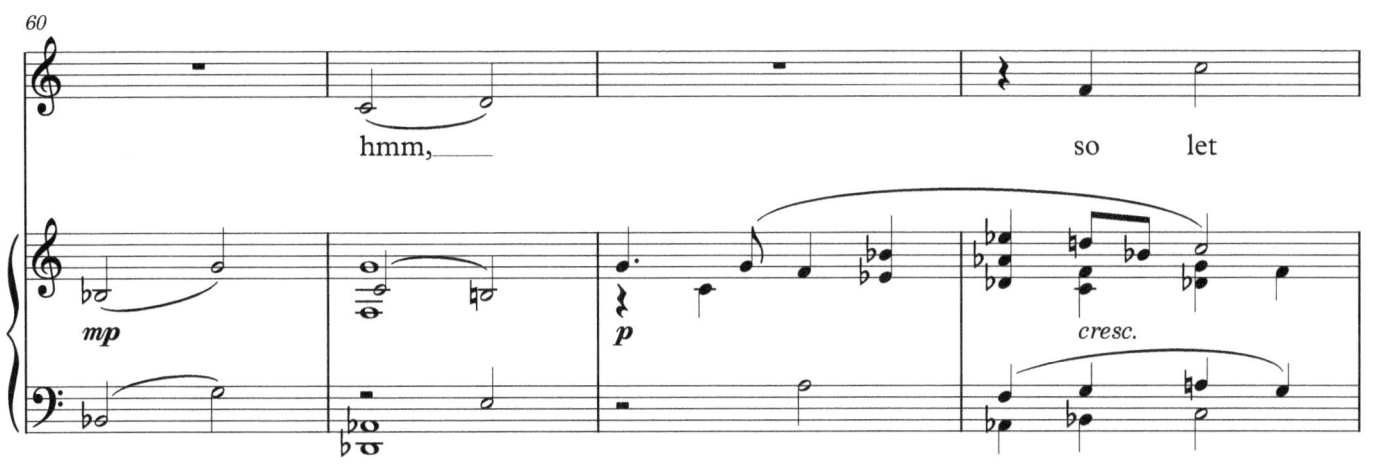
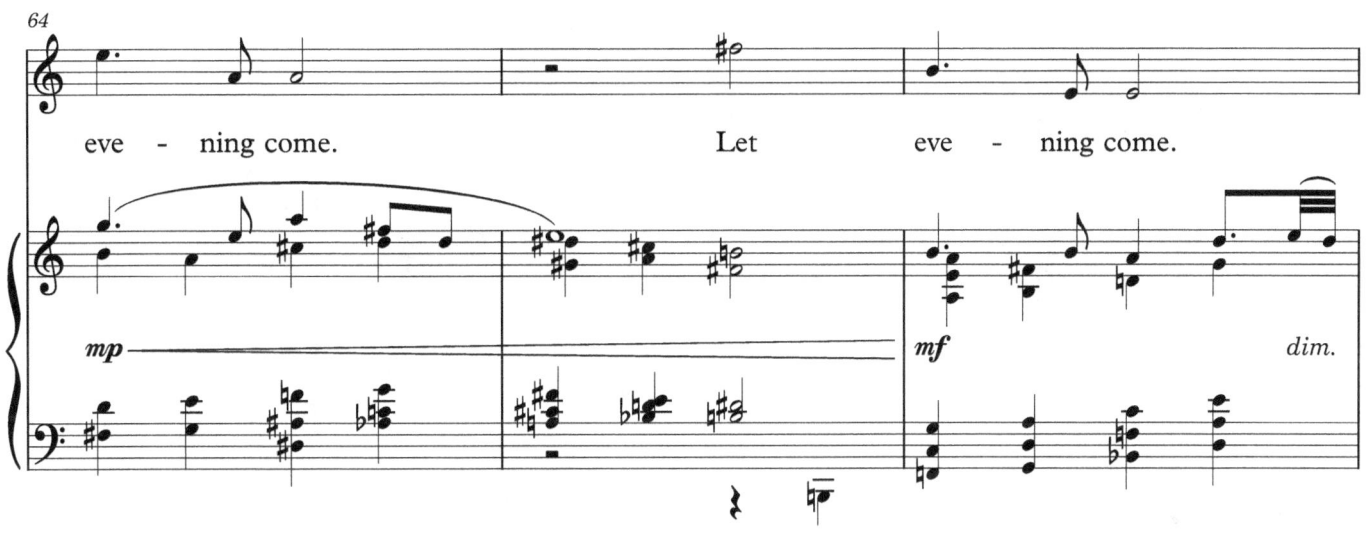
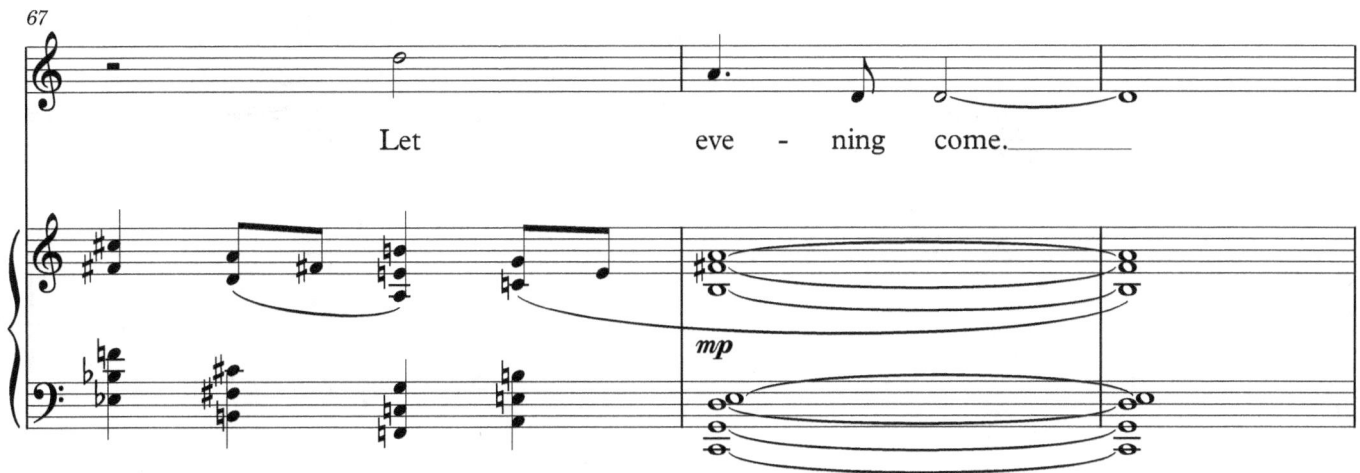

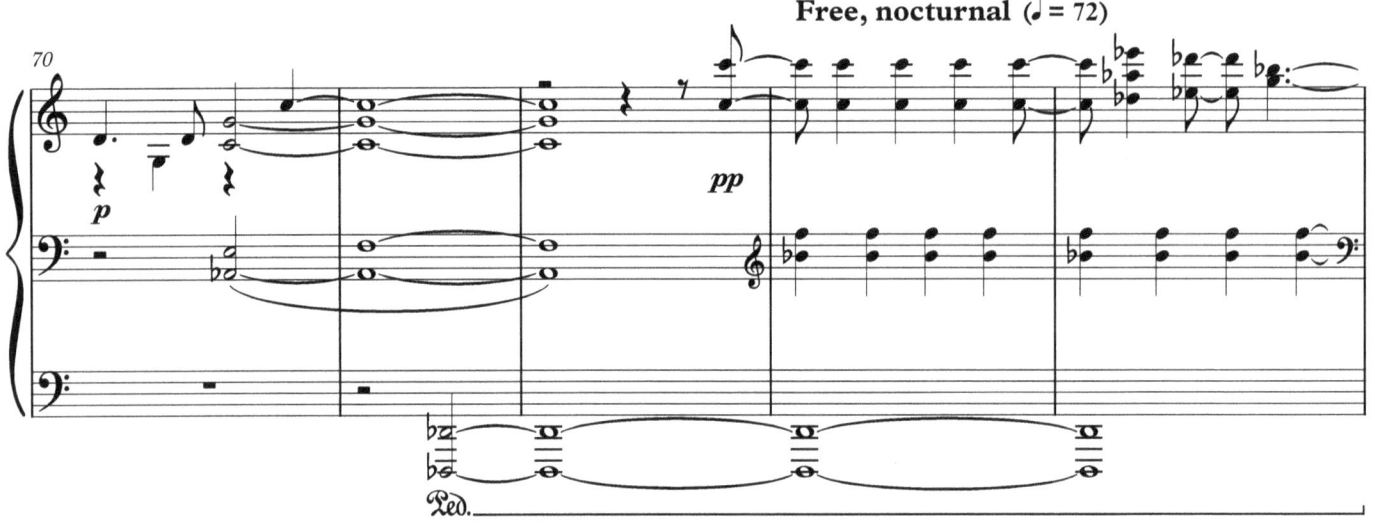

for Kayleigh Butcher and Christopher Narloch

Im Harren

STEFAN GEORGE

CARA HAXO
(2016)

In anticipation (♪ = c. 144)

Copyright © 2016 Cara Haxo (ASCAP).
All Rights Reserved.

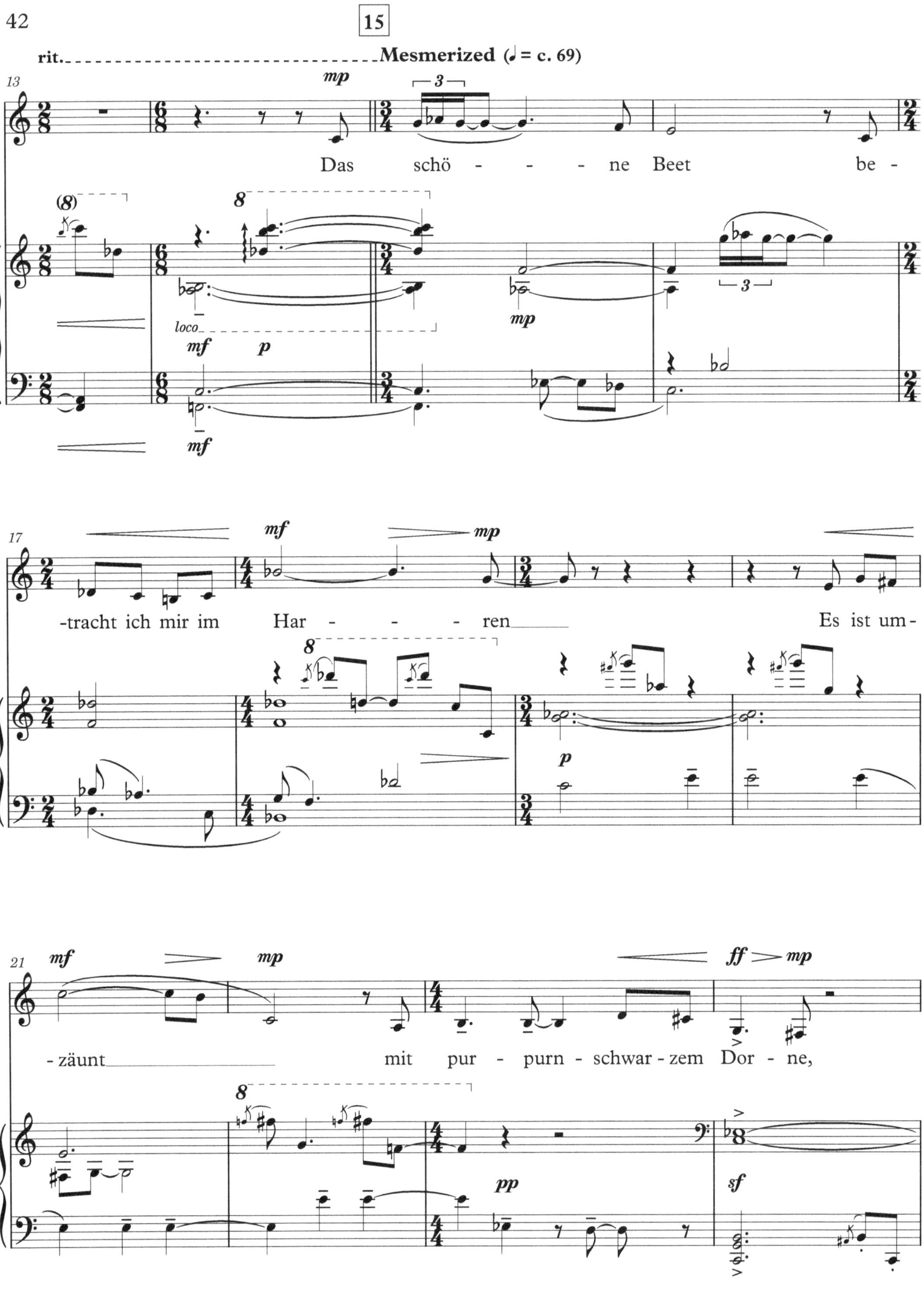

Death
from *Fragments of Solitude*

text from The Solitudes by LUIS DE GONGORIA
translated by EDITH GROSSMAN

CAMERON LAM
(2013)

Copyright © 2013 Cameron Lam. All Rights Reserved.

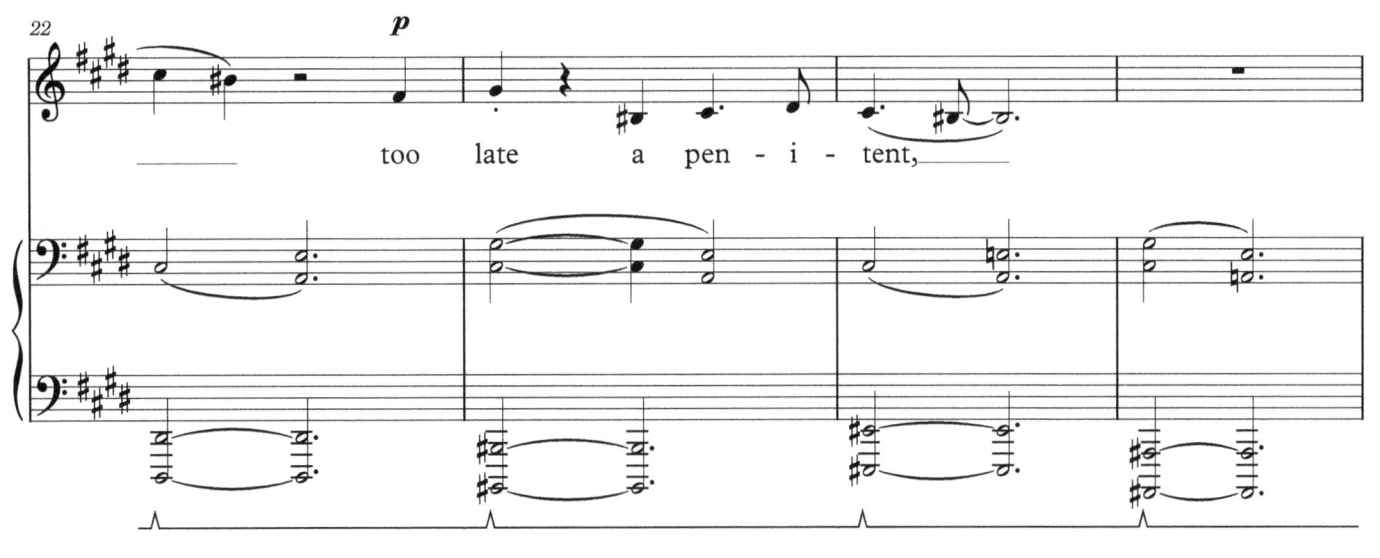
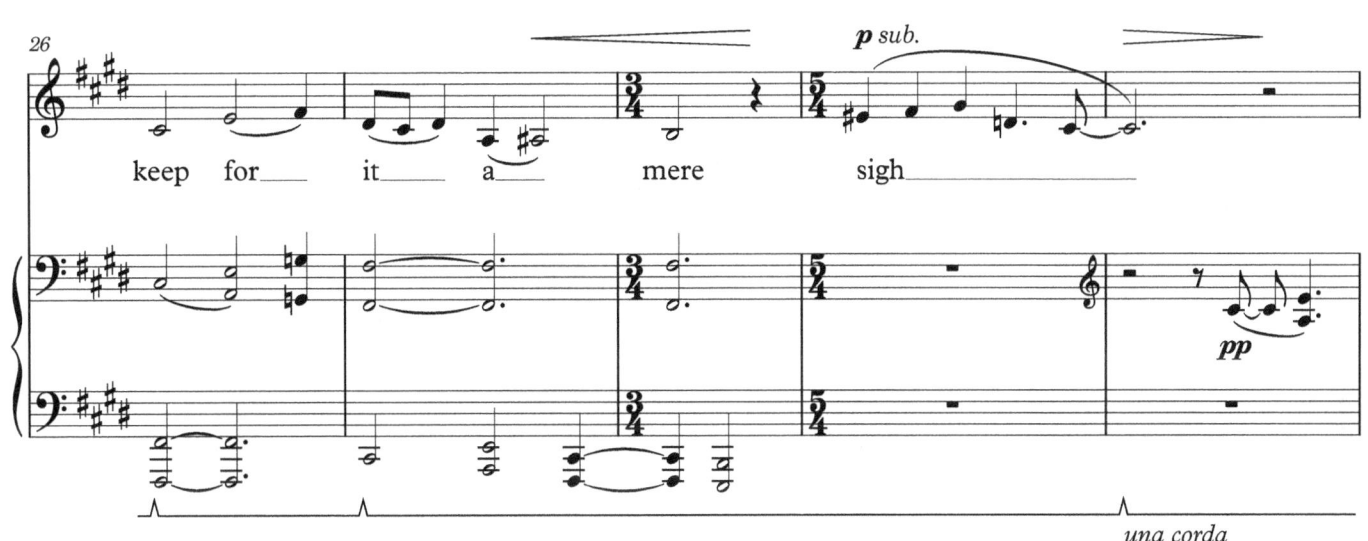

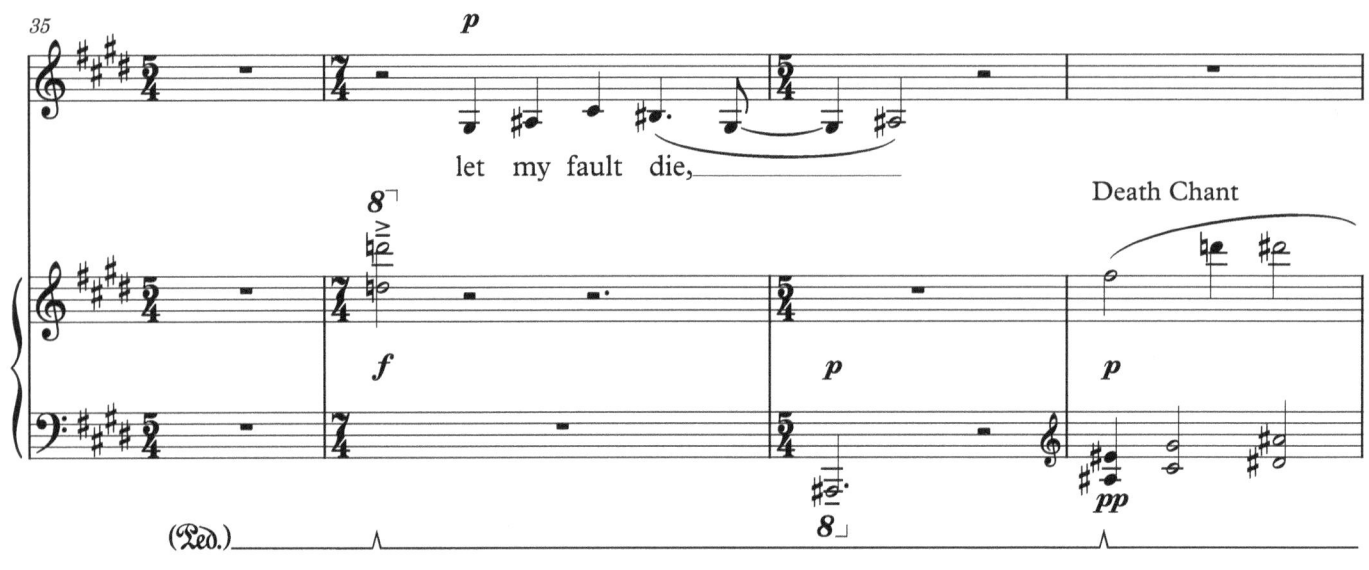

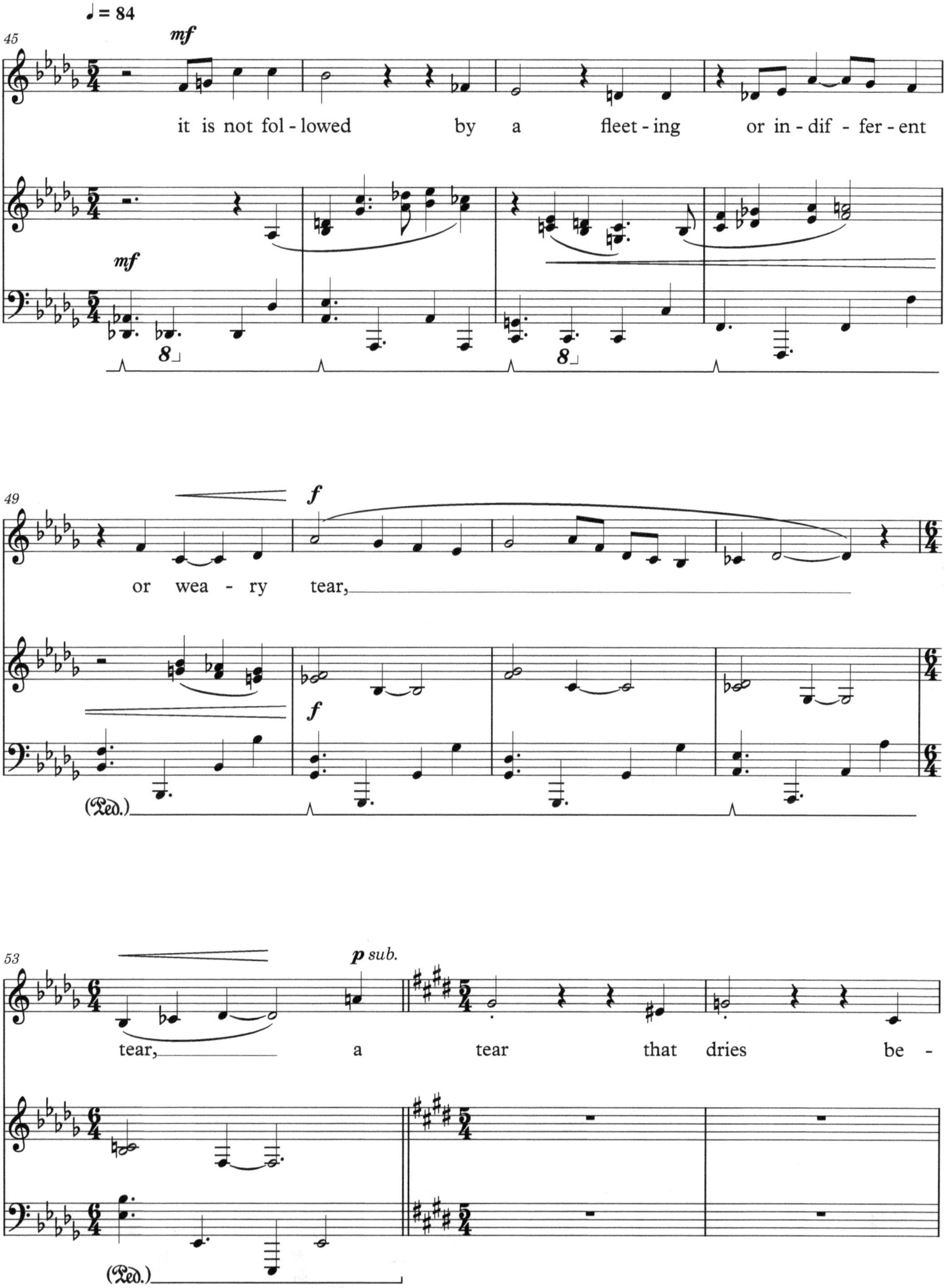

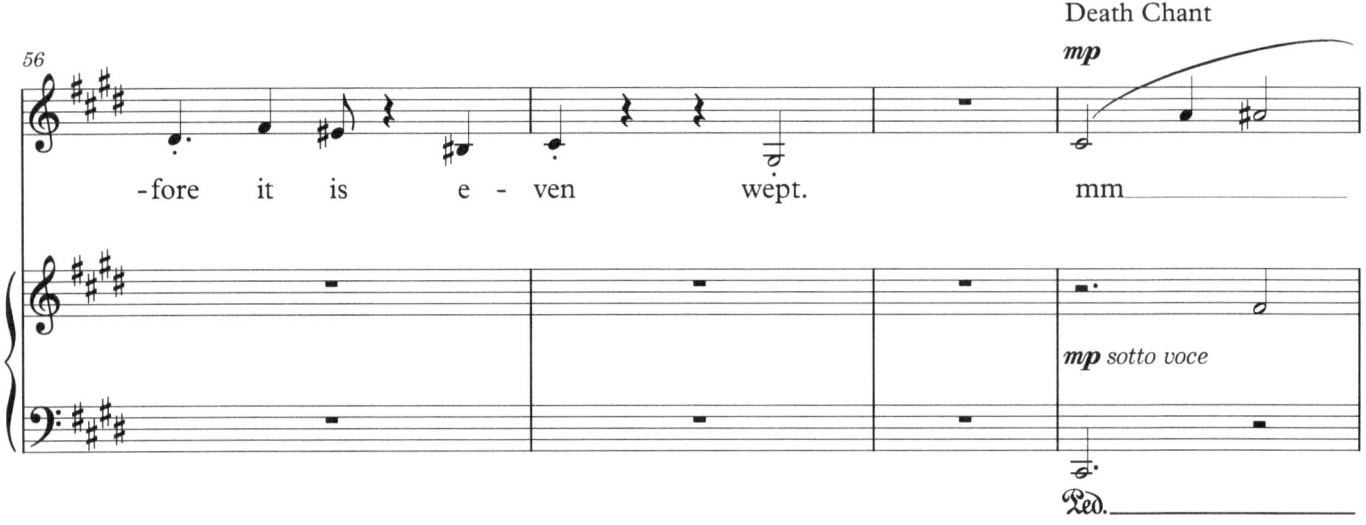
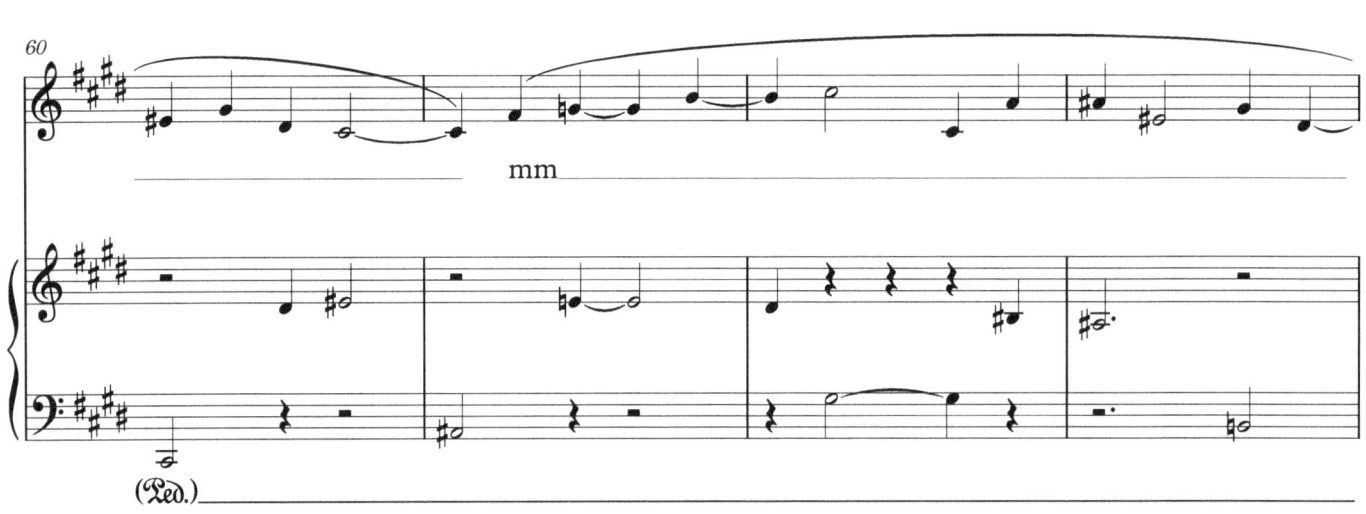

Give Me Your Hand

DUNCAN MACFARLANE

CECILIA LIVINGSTON
(2015)

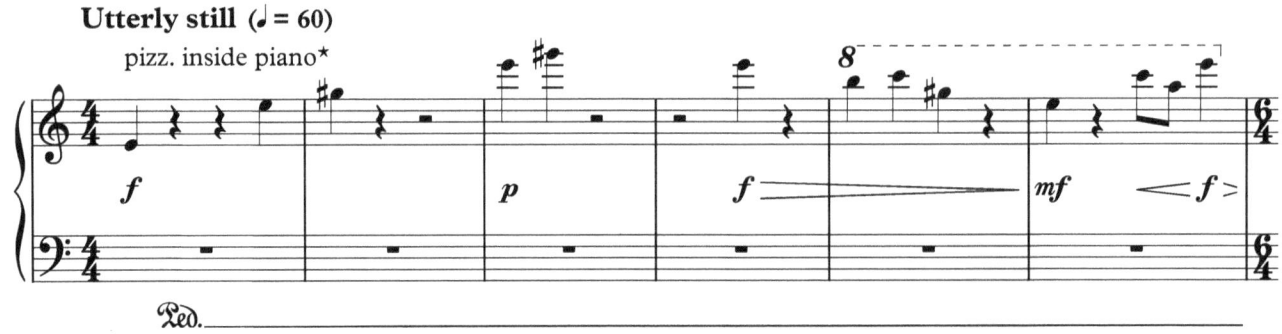

* pizz.: stand, plucking one of the strings for the given pitch with the fingernail (the piano becomes a very strange harp); L.V.

It may be helpful to remove the music rack and to label the hammers; a list/chart of the plucked notes is included as the last page of the score.

** The vocal line should be absolutely simple, with the rhythmic flexibility and freedom of Gregorian chant, so that the language drives the tempo (tenutos suggest text stress). Limpid, translucent, somewhere between a chant, a lullaby, and a bereft lament, is hould ache with loneliness.

Grace notes should feel "on the beat."

* Hold keys with diamond noteheads down with fingers; do not release the keys.

** Once the resonance has been "caught" in the new pedaling, stand and release the held keys, keeping the "new" pedal down.

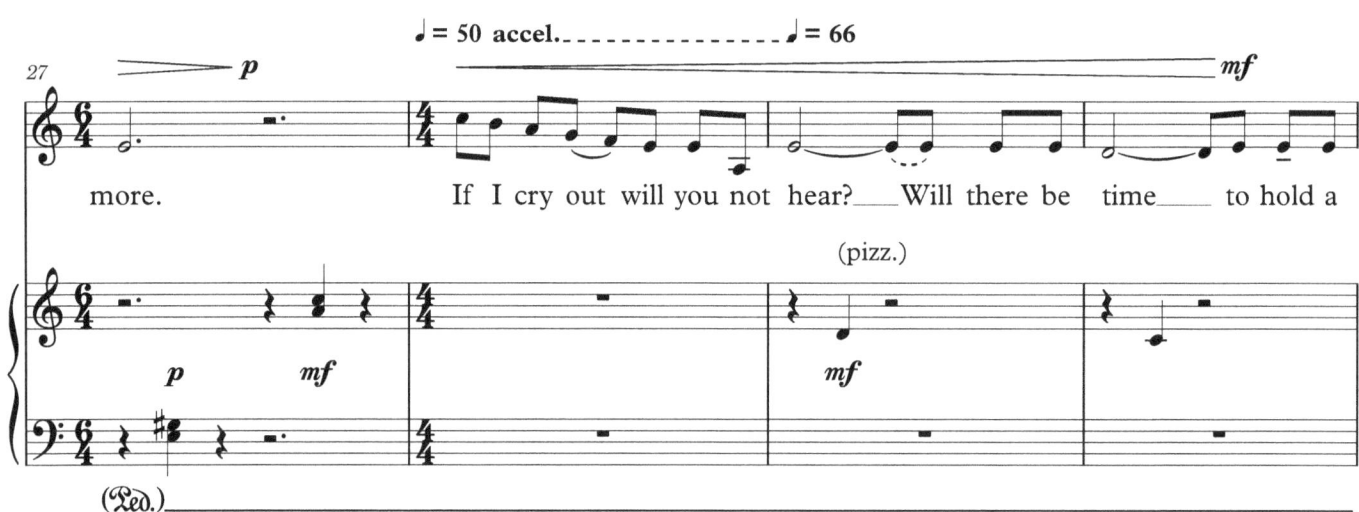
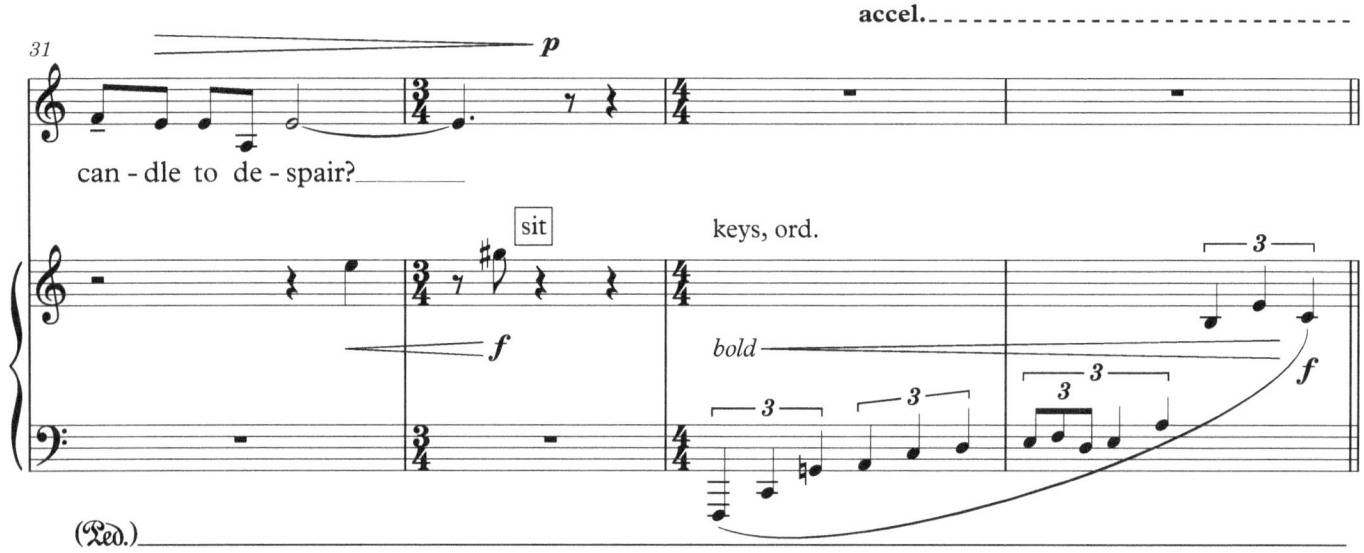

*accel. so that the triplet quarters flow directly into the eighth notes.

** As the decay fades, stand and release the held keys, keeping the pedal down

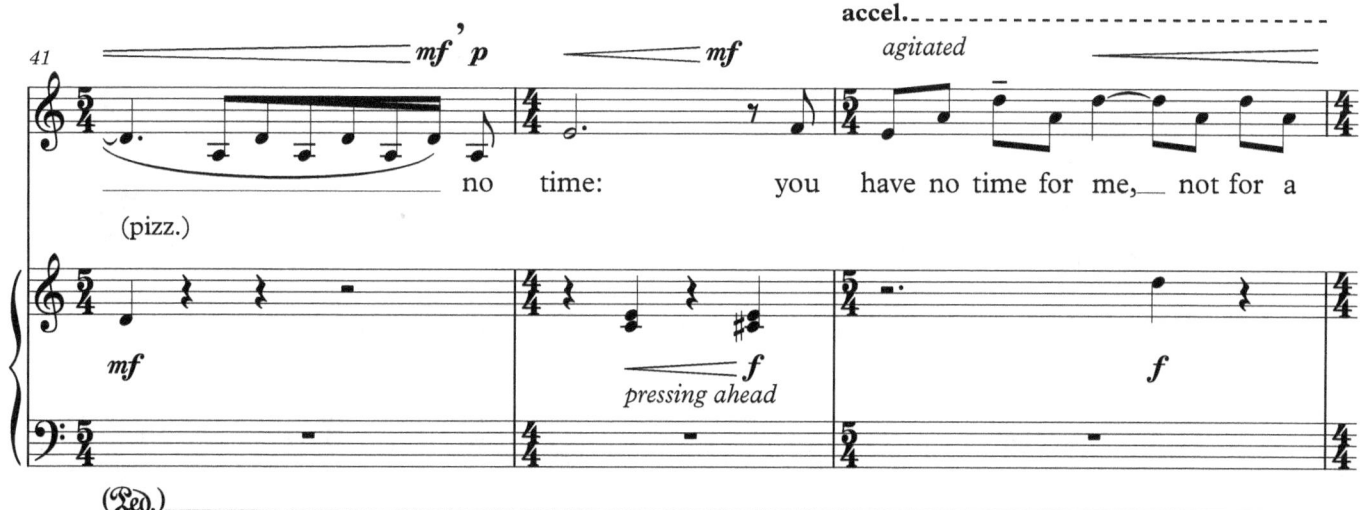

* Once the resonance has been "caught" in the new pedaling, stand and release the held keys, keeping the "new" pedal down.

** As the decay fades, stand and release the held keys, keeping the pedal down

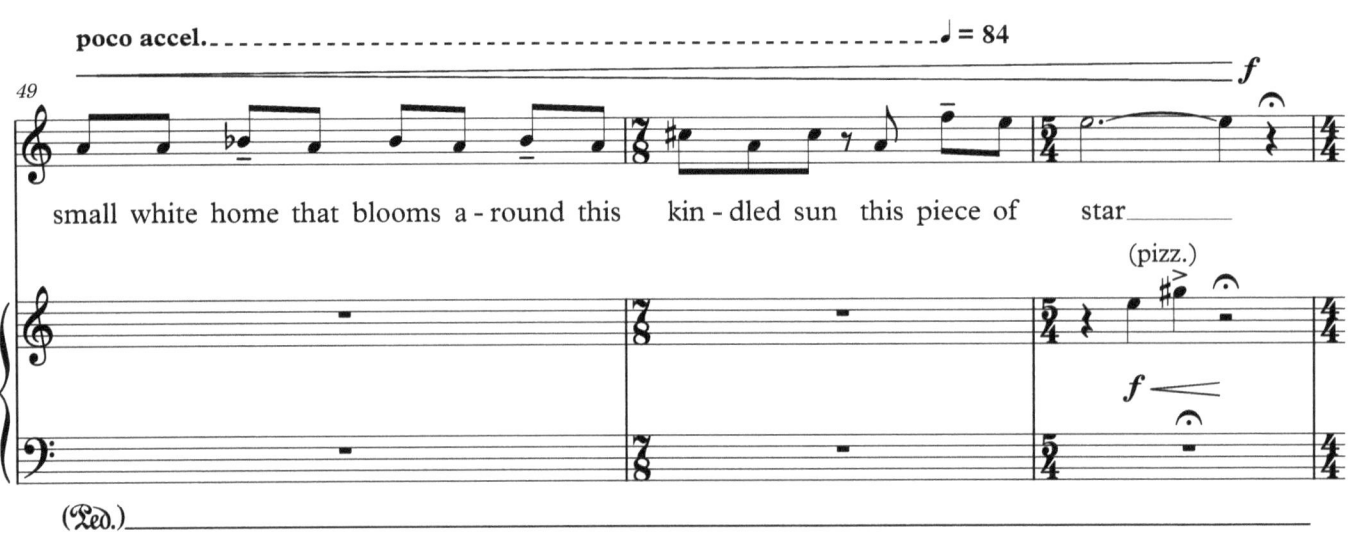

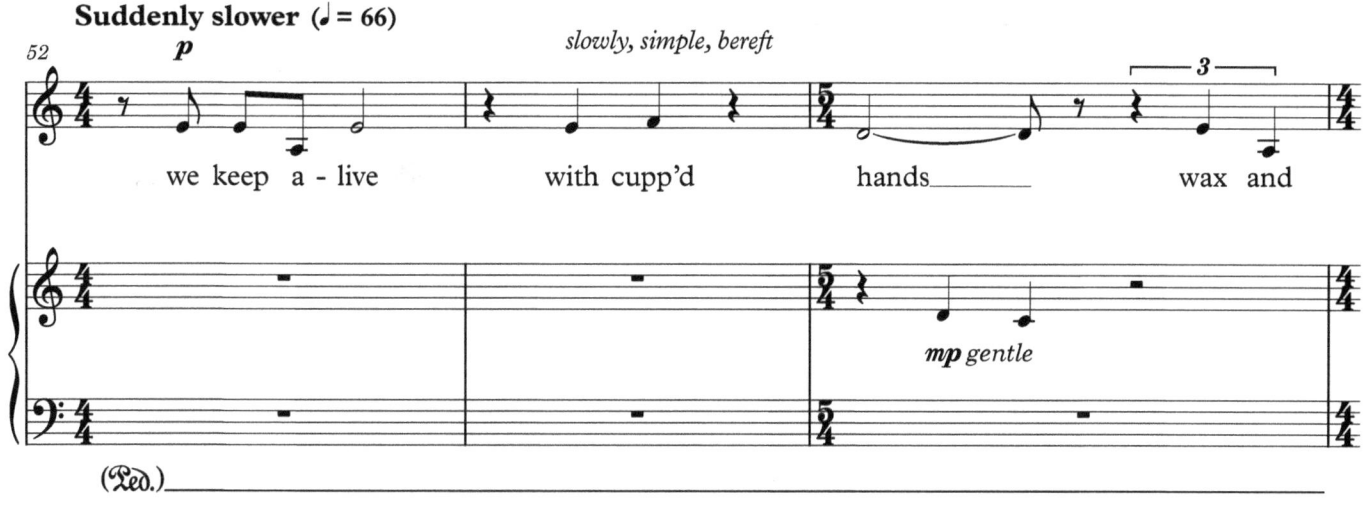

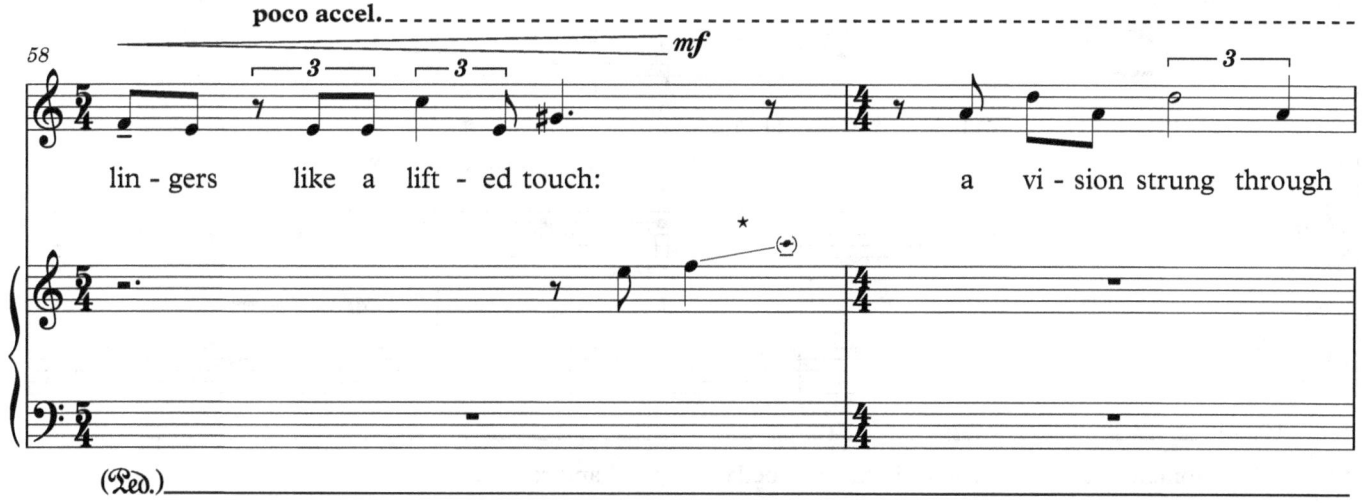

* Pluck, then drag the fingertip across the strings

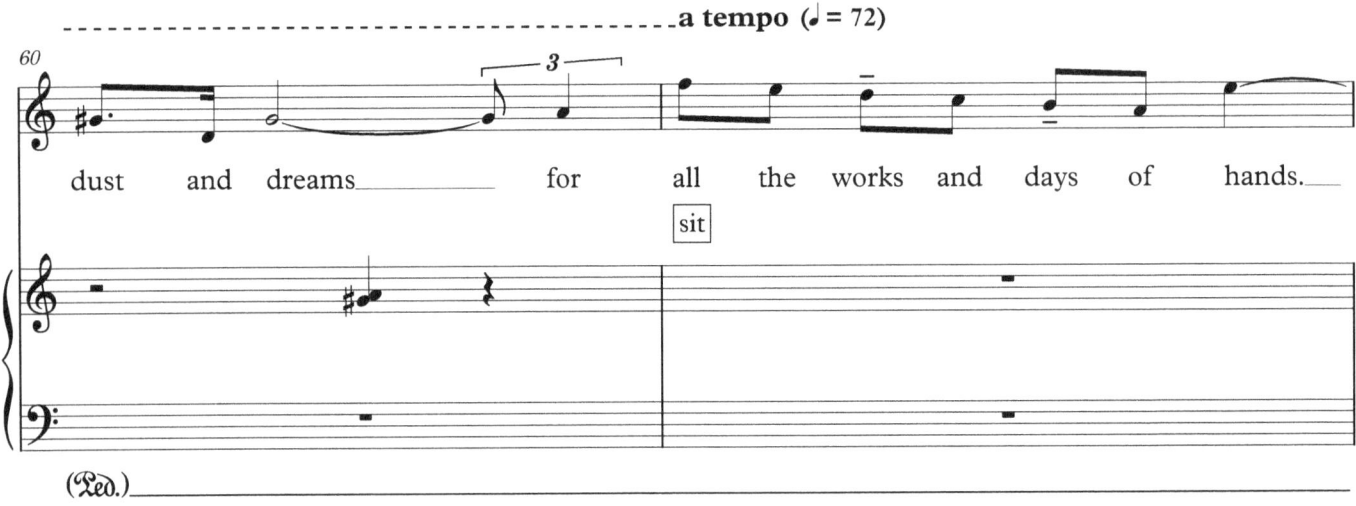

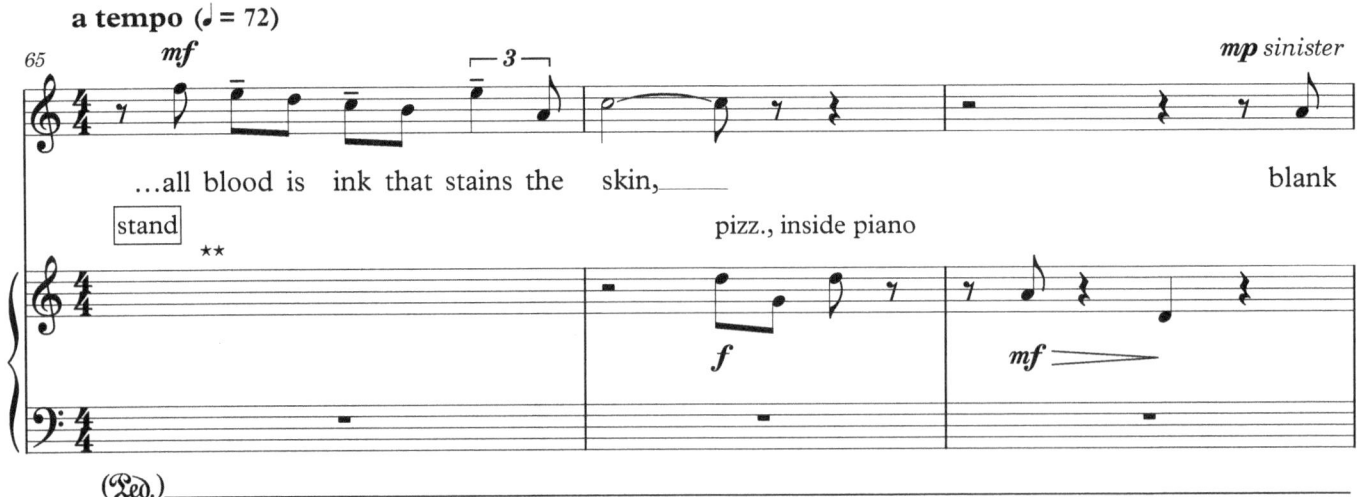

* Once the resonance has been "caught" in the new pedaling, stand and release the held keys, keeping the "new" pedal down.

** As the decay fades, stand and release the held keys, keeping the pedal down

* Pluck, then drag the fingertip across the strings

** Once the resonance has been "caught" in the new pedaling, stand and release the held keys, keeping the "new" pedal down.

* As the decay fades, stand and release the held keys, keeping the pedal down

Give Me Your Hand
Plucked Strings

The pianist may wish to label the hammers for the plucked notes.

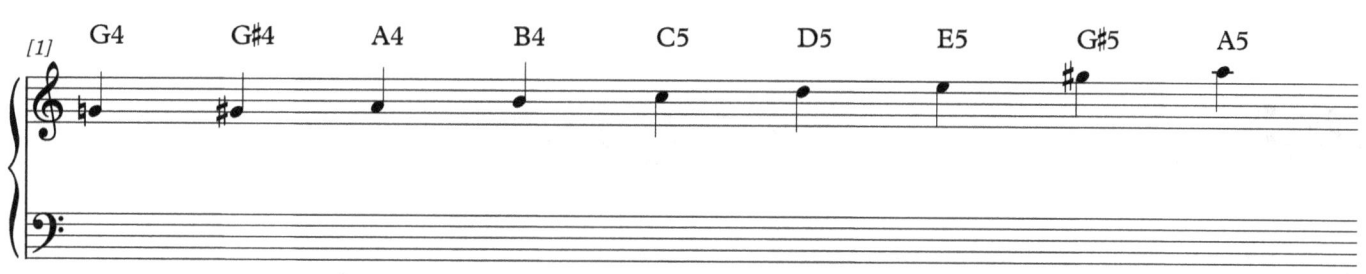

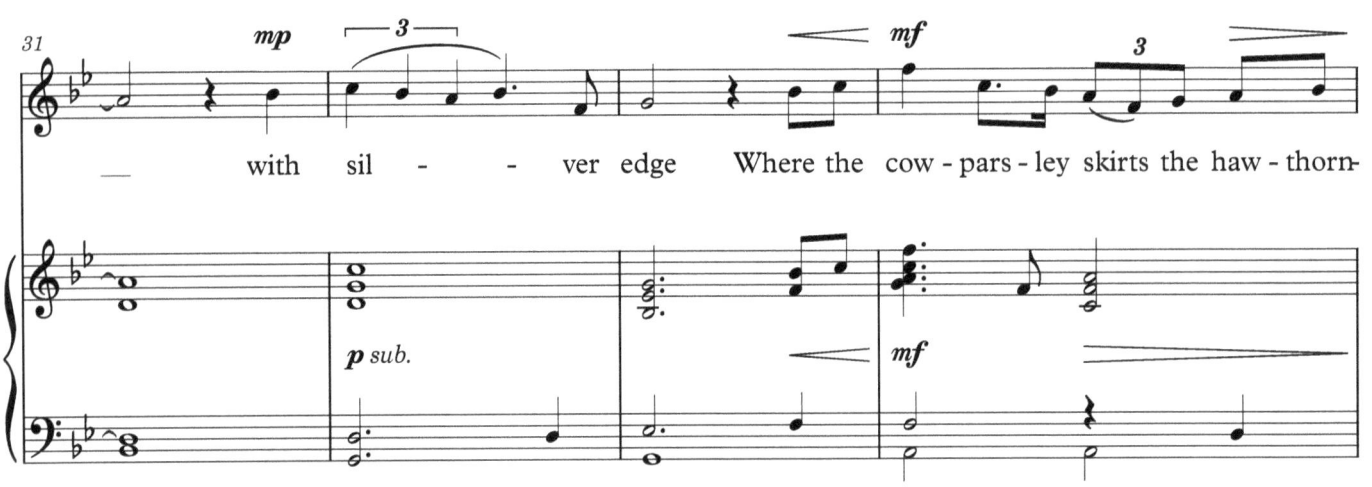
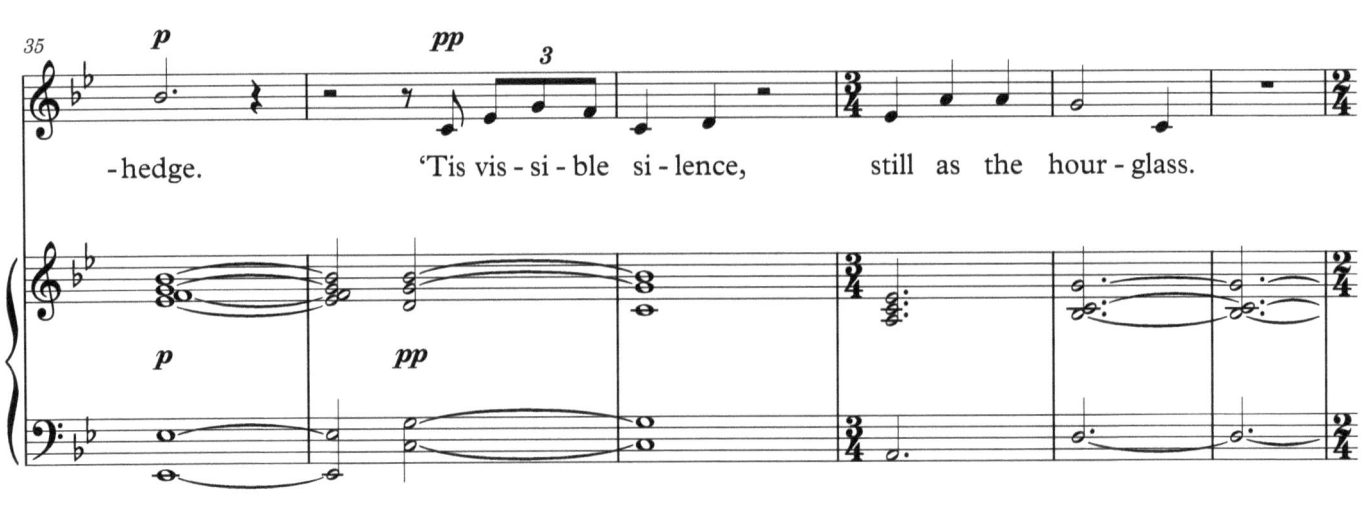

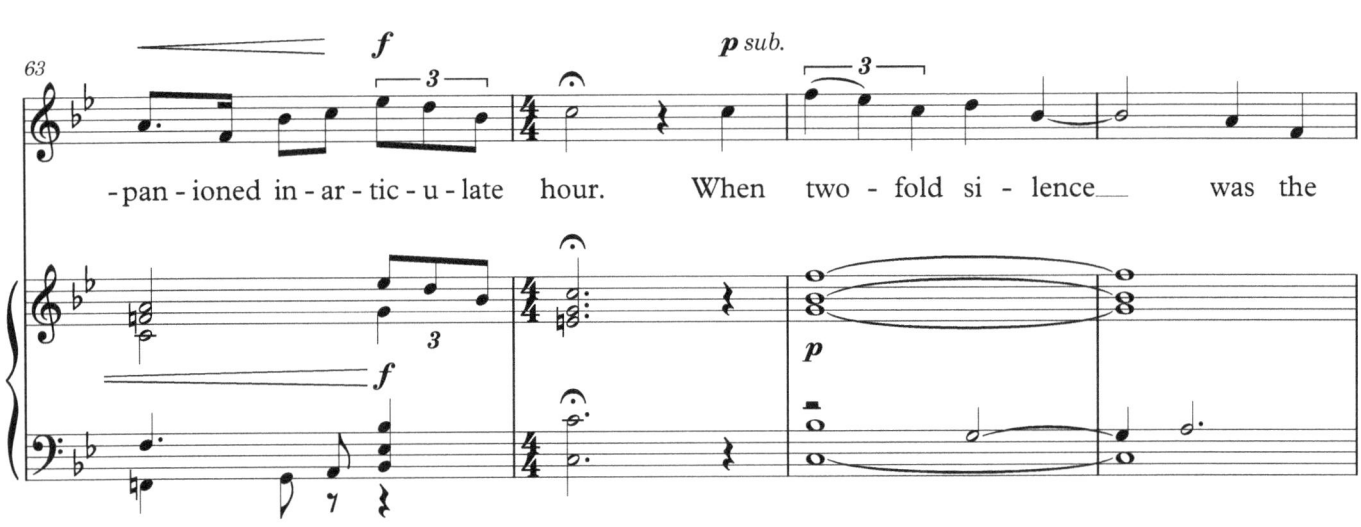

to Megan Ihnen
Prairie Dawn

WILLA CATHER

TONY MANFREDONIA
(2017)

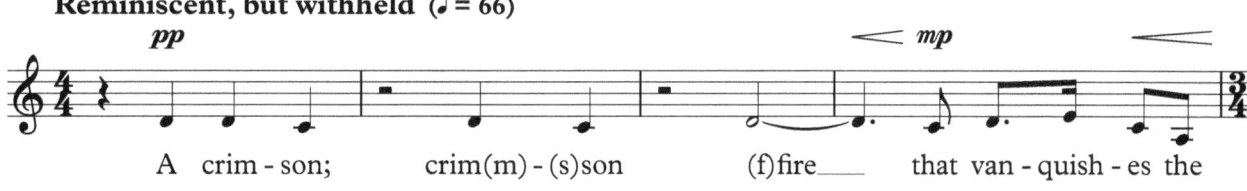

♪ = closer to speaking than singing

♩ = whispered in general range of pitches

Copyright © 2017 Tony Manfredonia (BMI). All Rights Reserved.

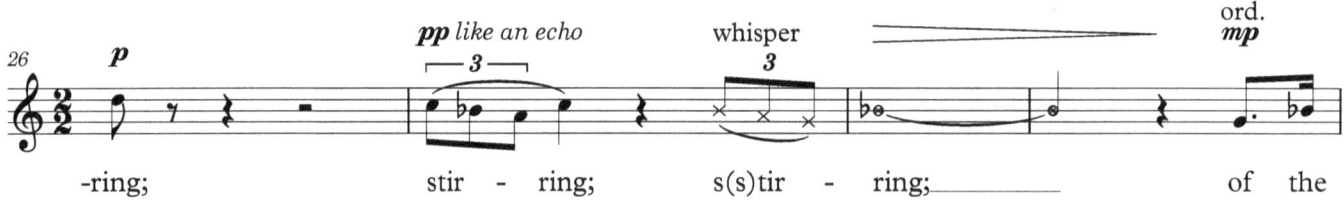
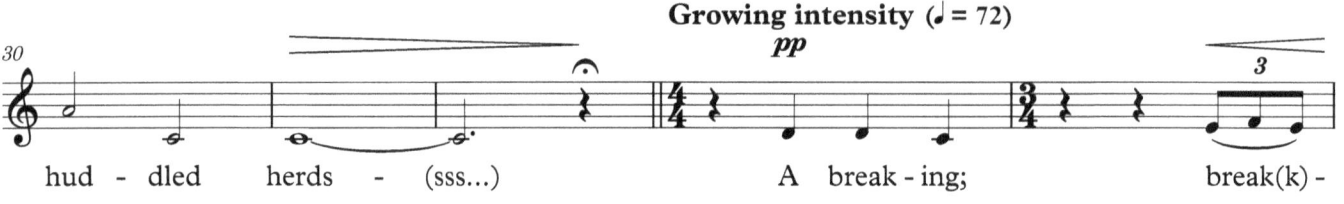
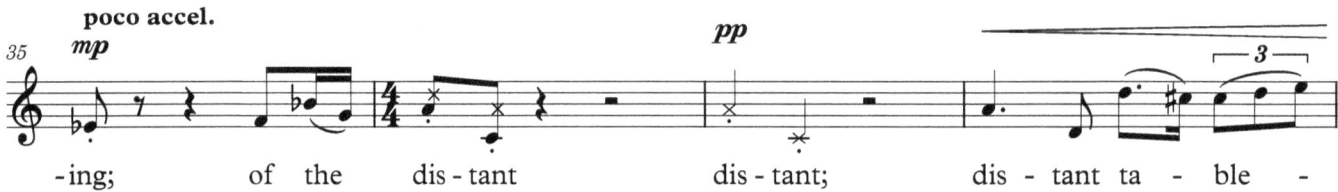
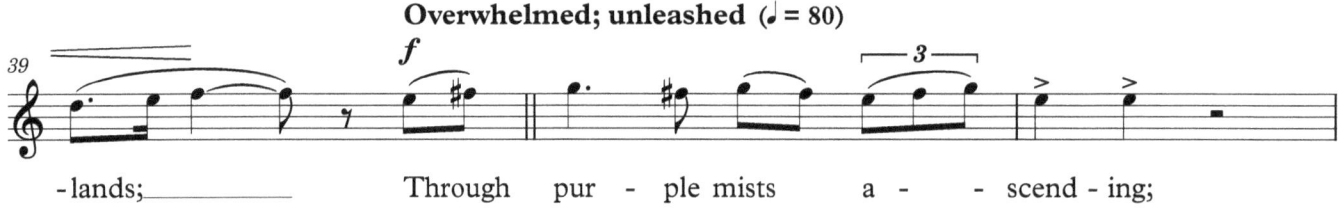

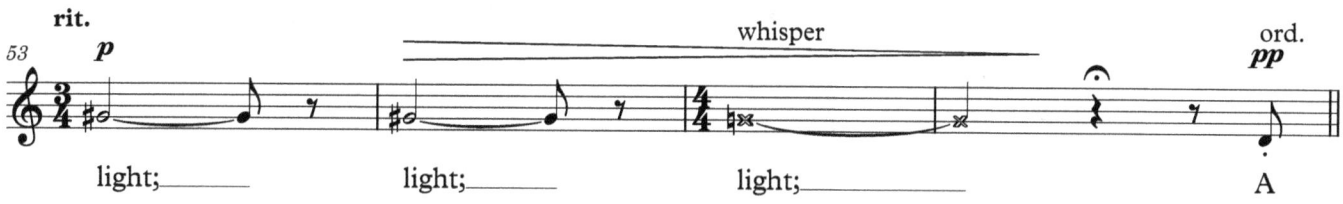

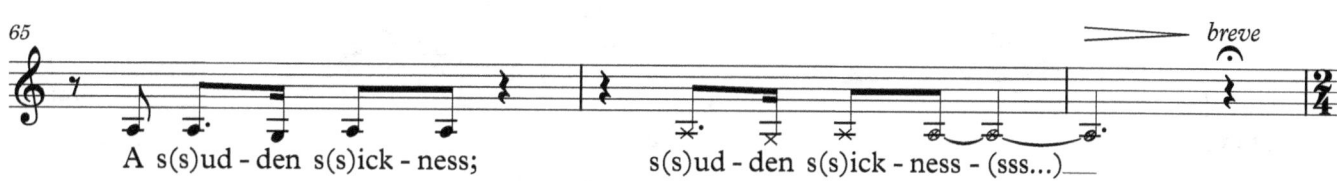
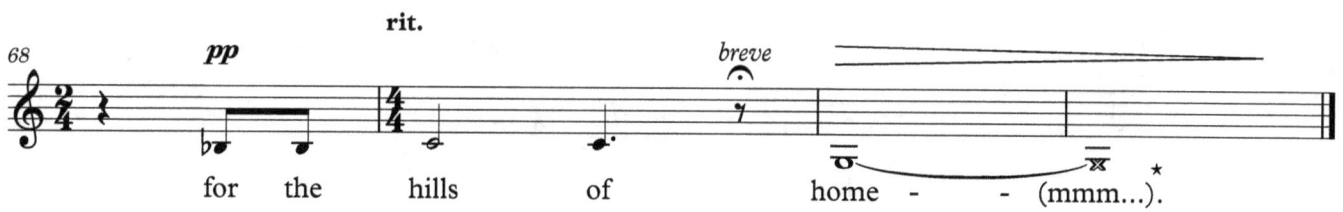

* Exhaling closed "m" in a whisper

air stirs

BASHŌ

April's air stirs in
willow-leaves... A butterfly
floats and balances

NICOLE MURPHY
(2015)

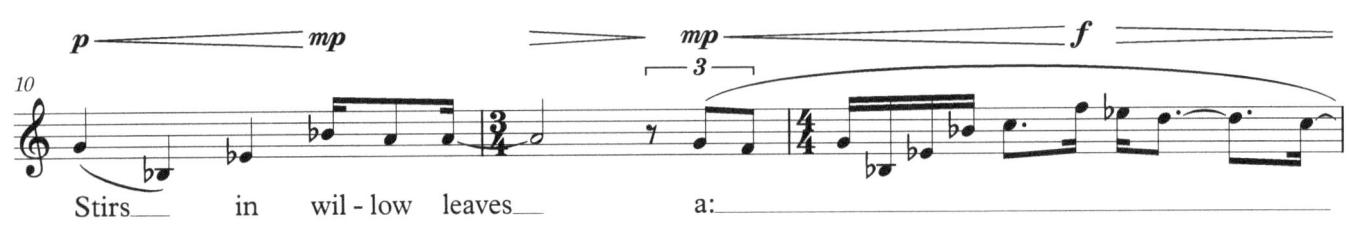

Copyright © Nicole Murphy 2015. All Rights Reserved.

Thief's Song
from *The Accidental Feast of the Holy Fool*

JANE YOLEN

ERIC PAZDZIORA
(2013)

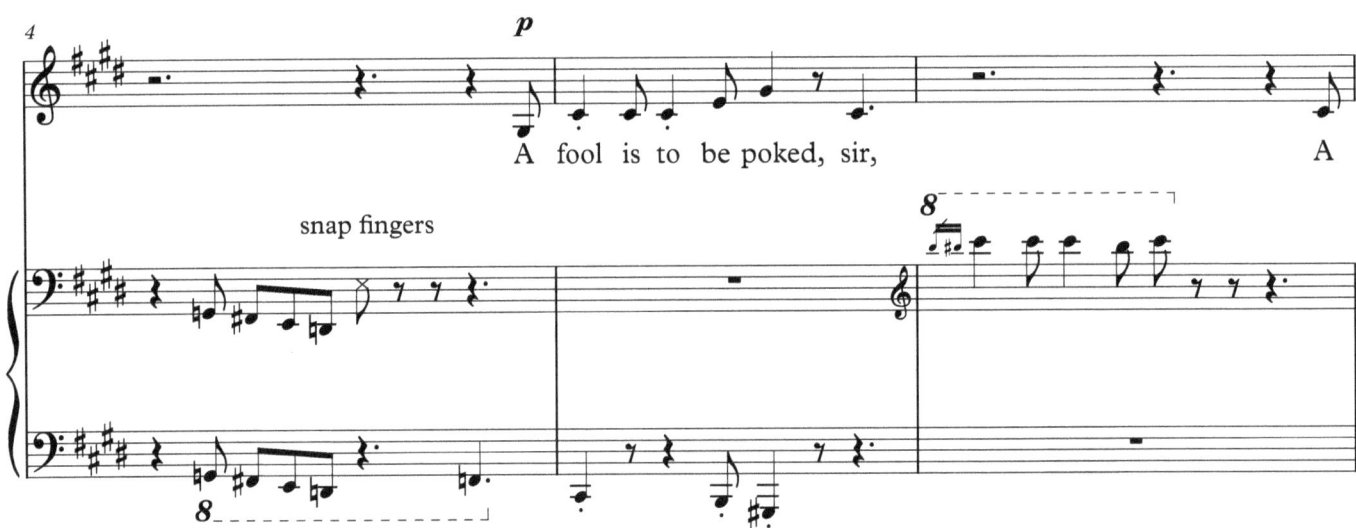

Music Copyright © 2013 Eric Pazdziora.
Words Copyright © 2013 Jane Yolen.

74

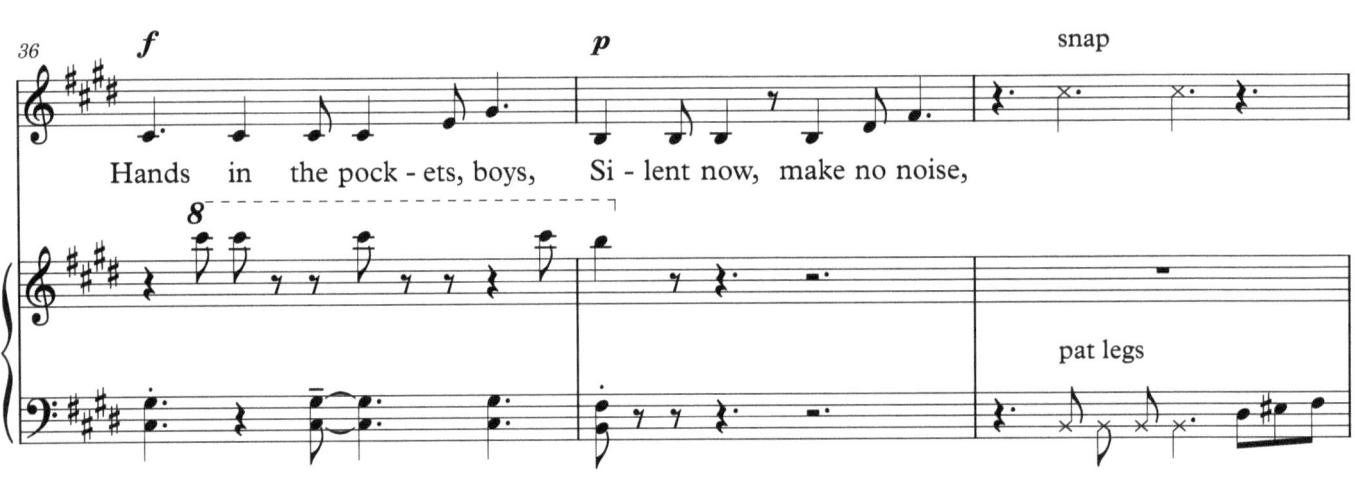

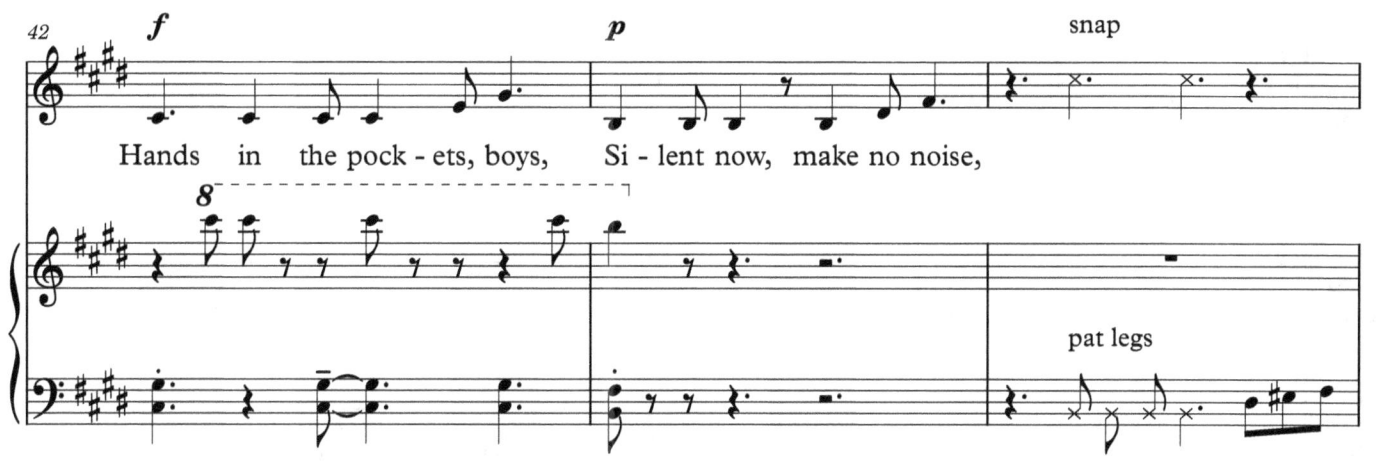

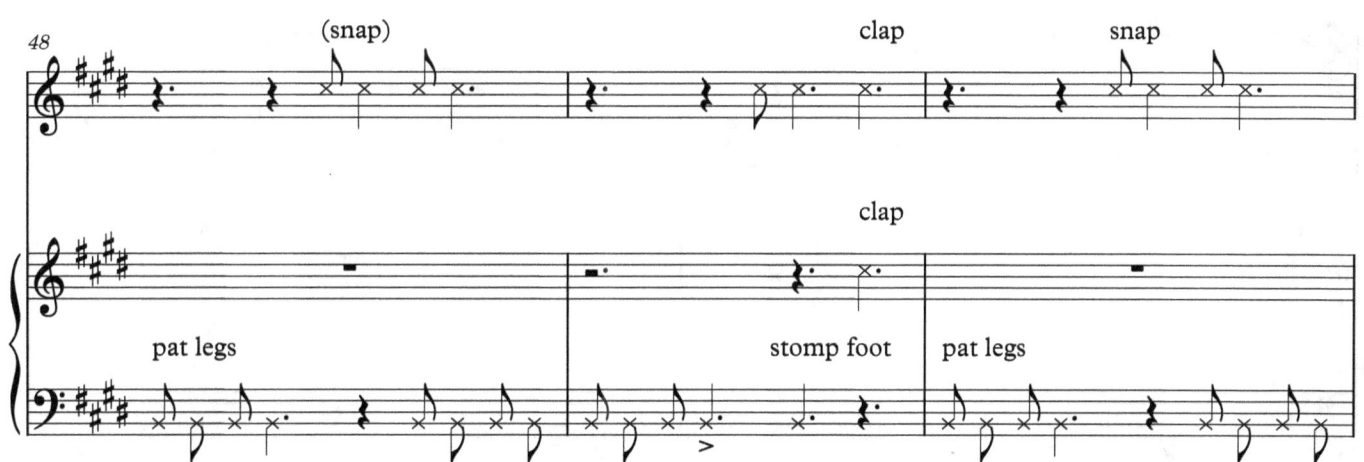

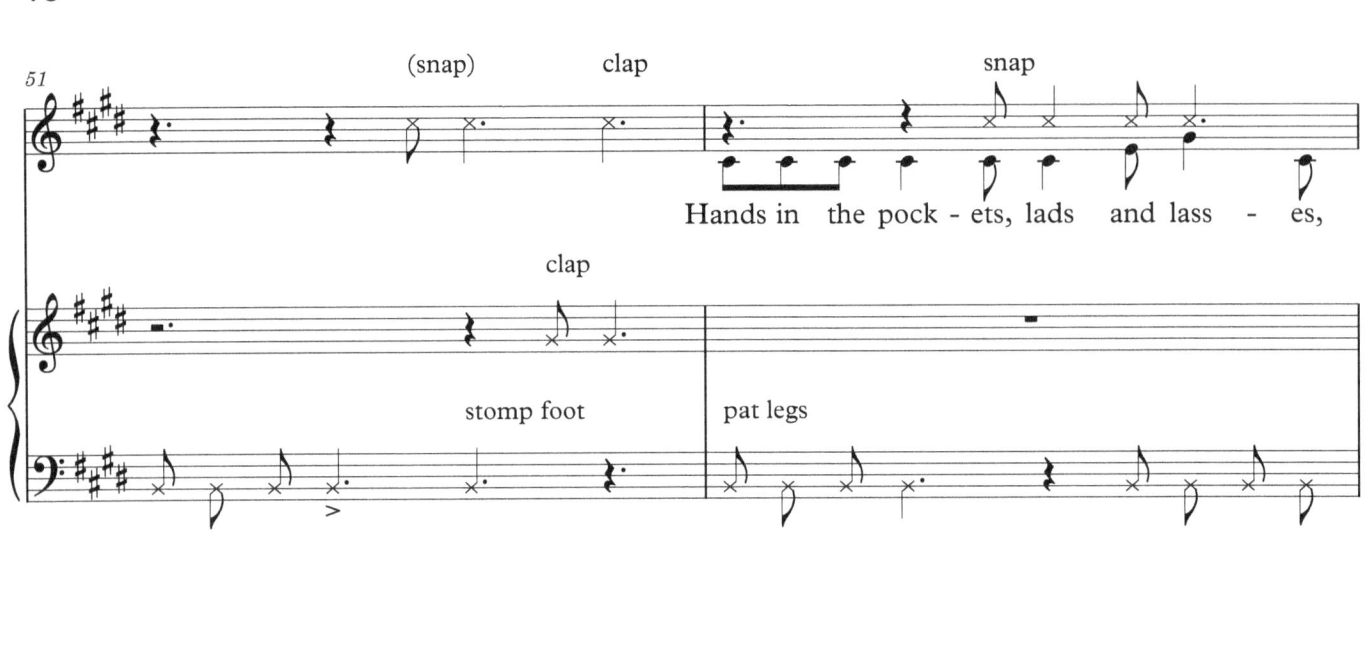
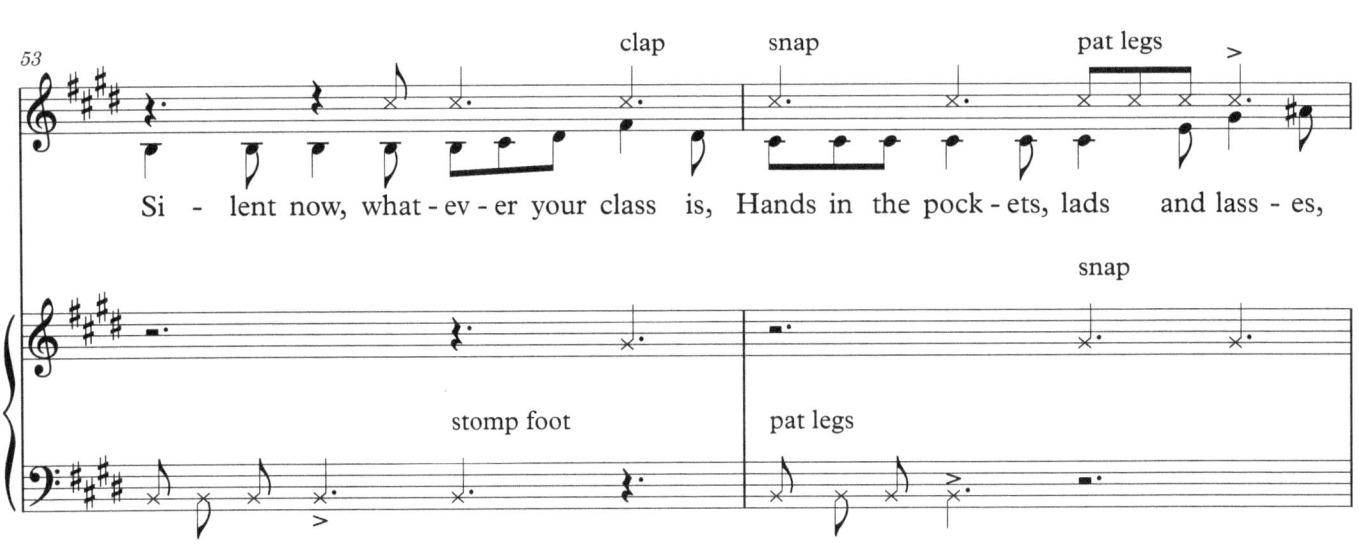
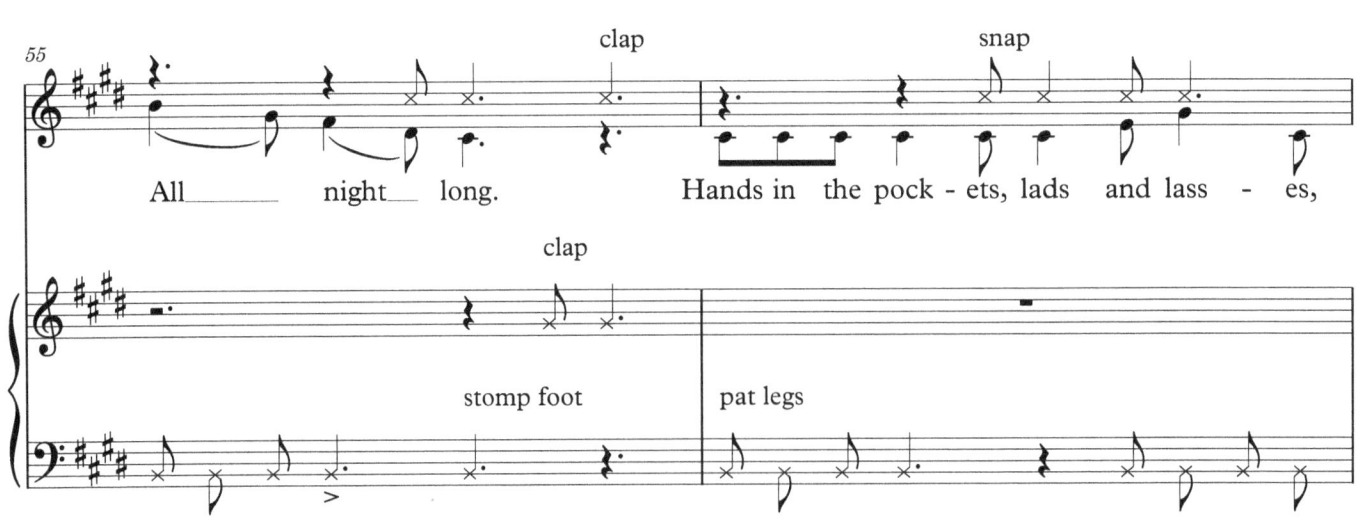

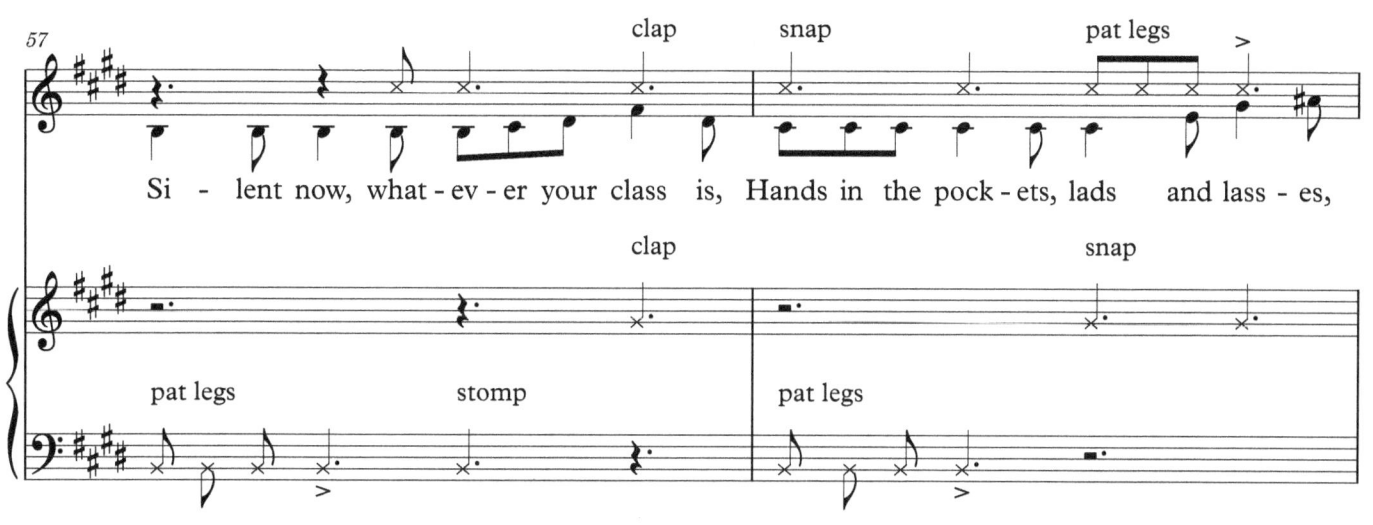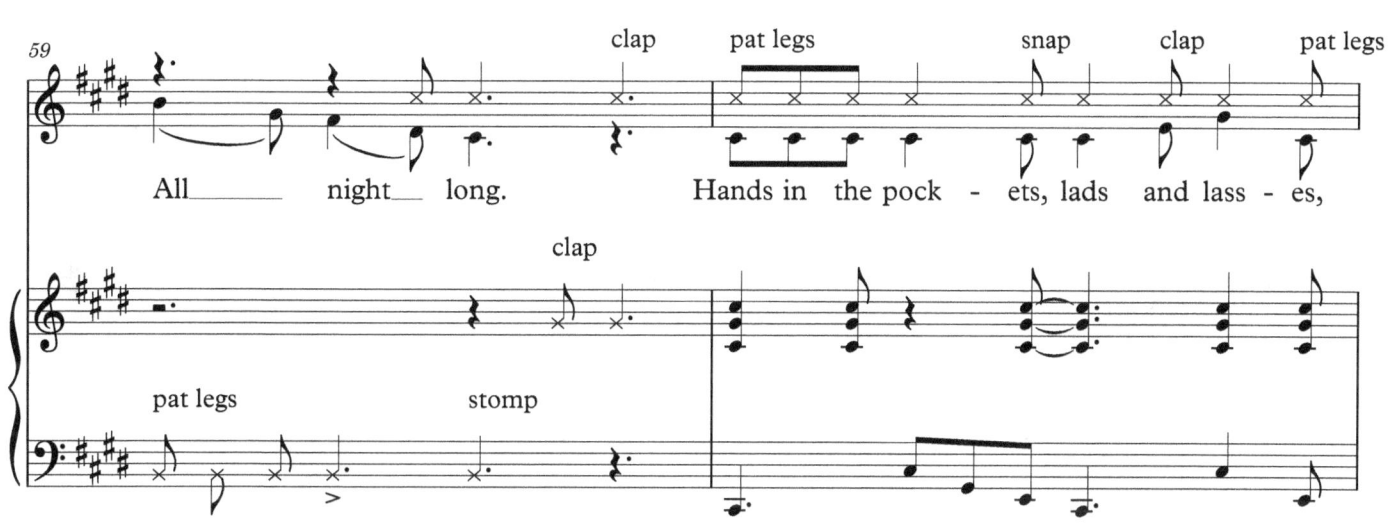

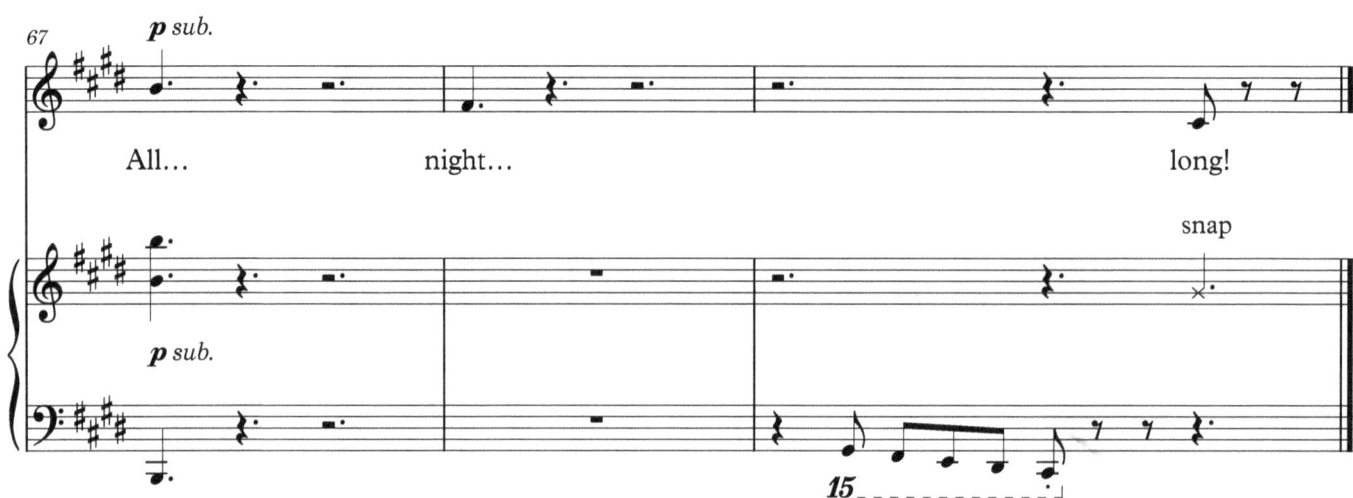

for Jillian
Scheherazade

RICHARD SIKEN FRANCES POLLOCK
(2017)

Copyright © 2017 Frances Pollock. All Rights Reserved.
francespollockmusic@gmail.com

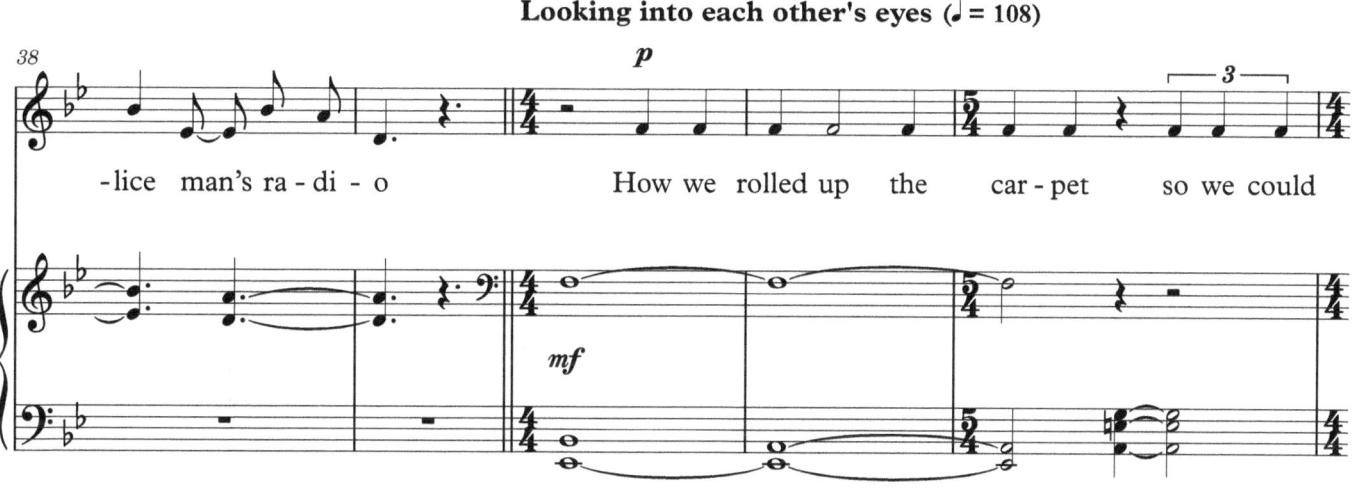
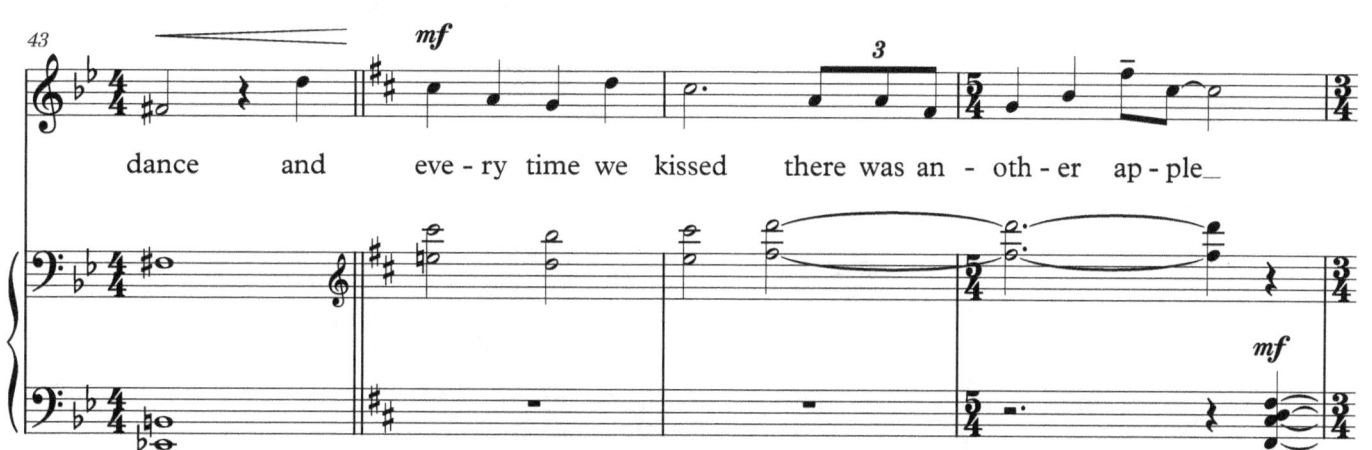

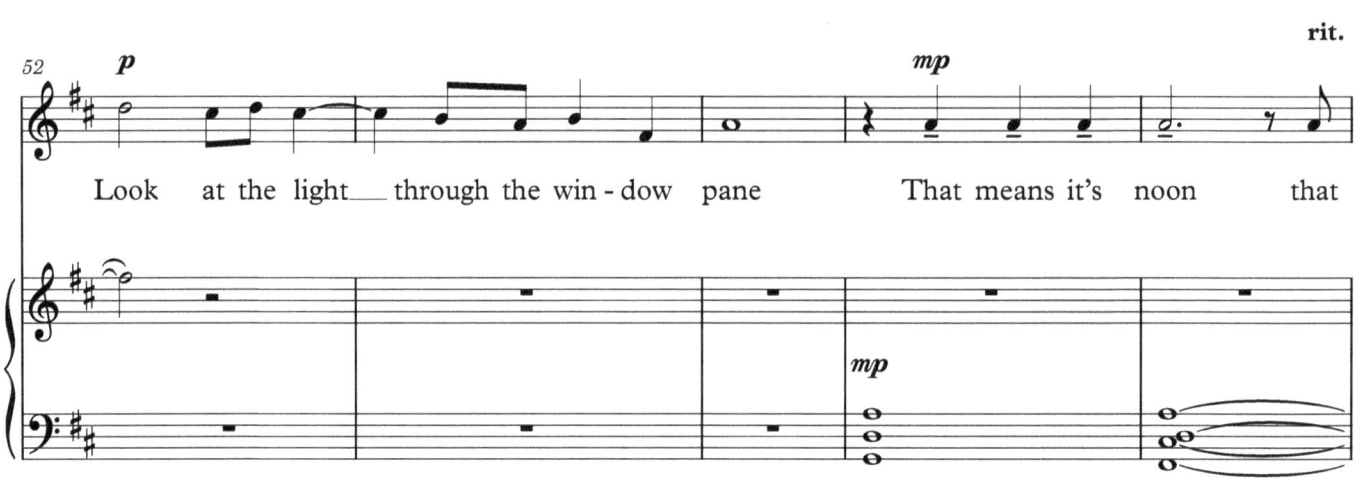
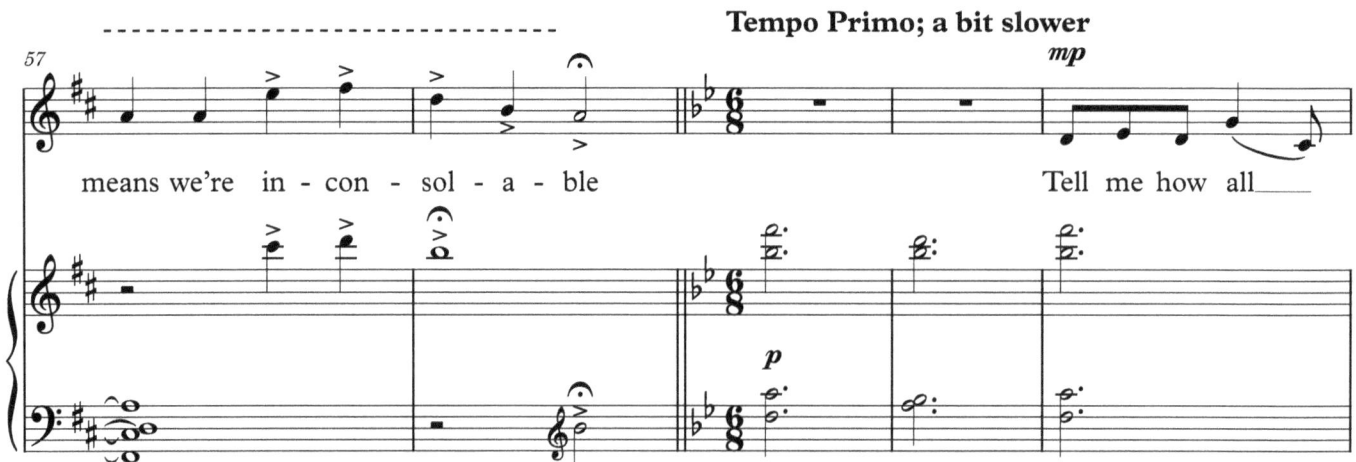

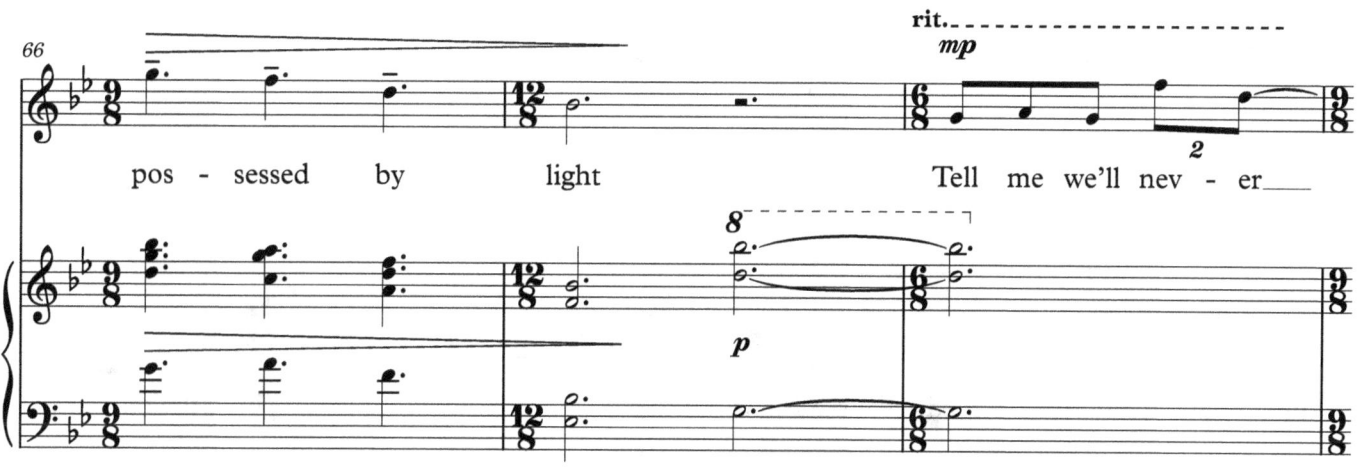
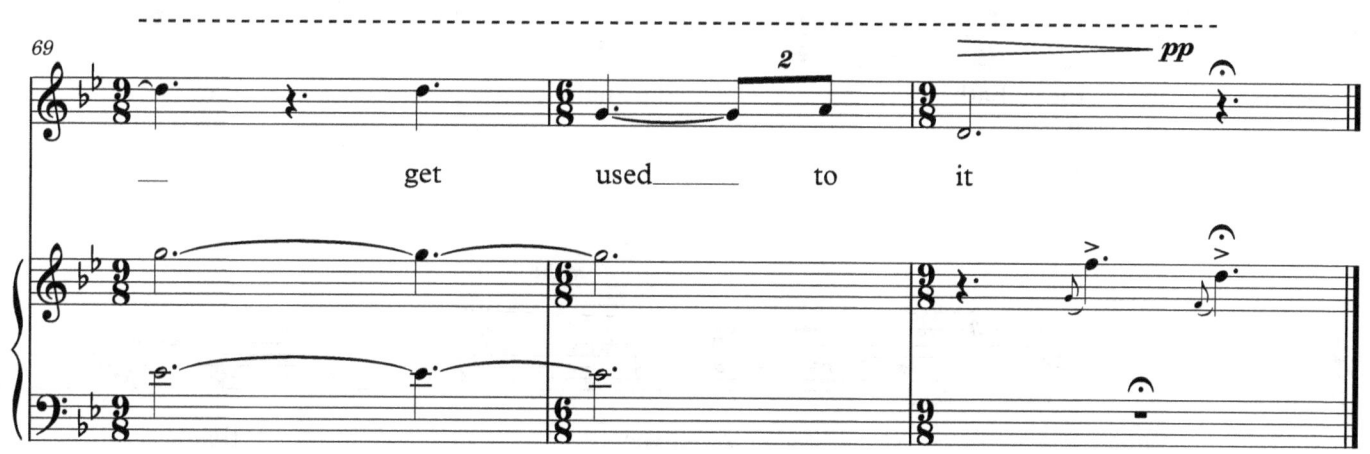

Prayer at my parting
from *Portraits of Disquiet*

KENDALL A.

JULIA SEEHOLZER
(2016)

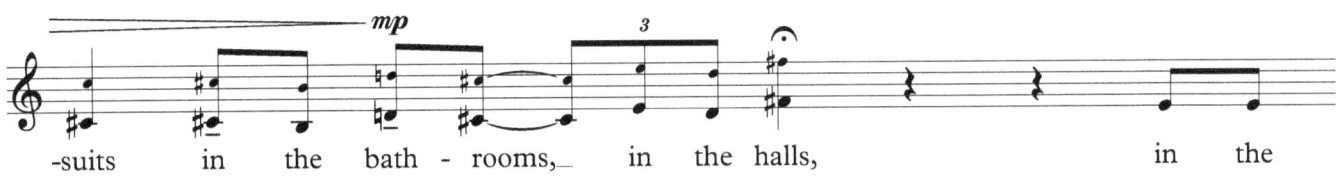

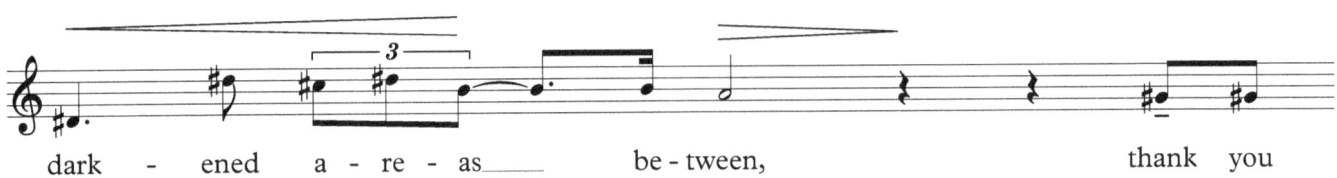

Copyright © 2016 Julia Seeholzer & Kendall A.

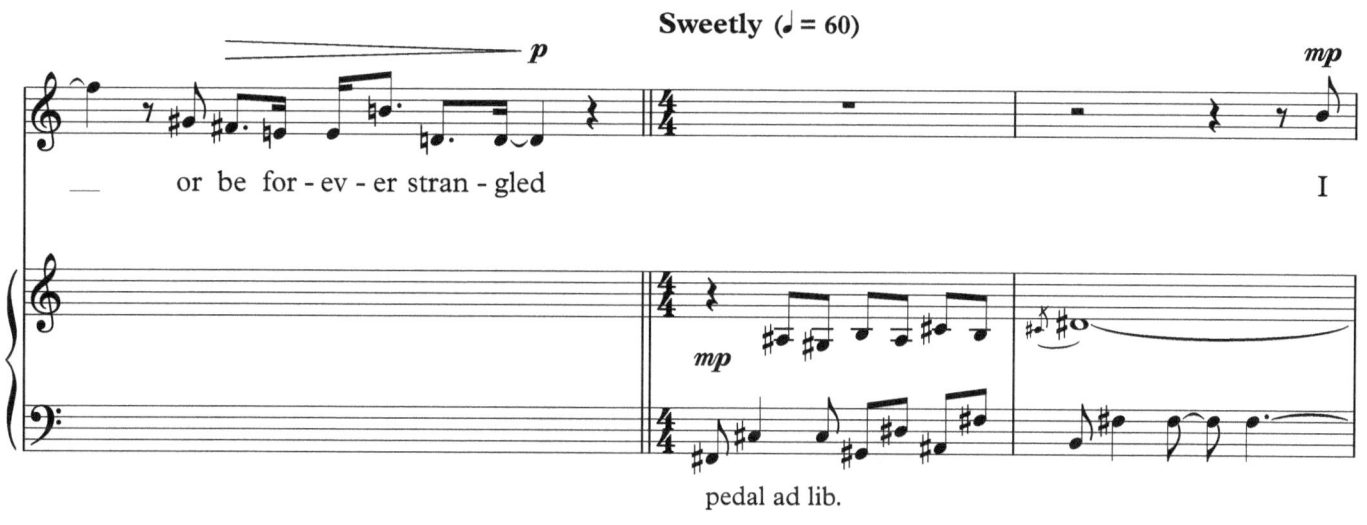
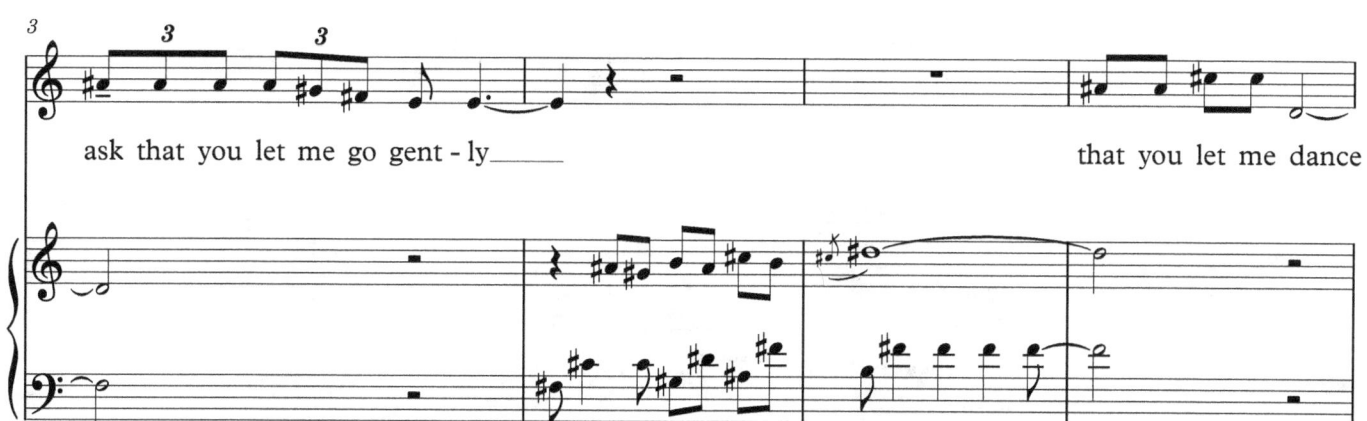

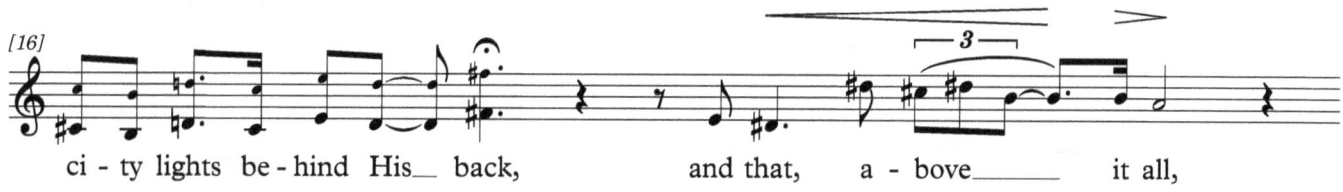

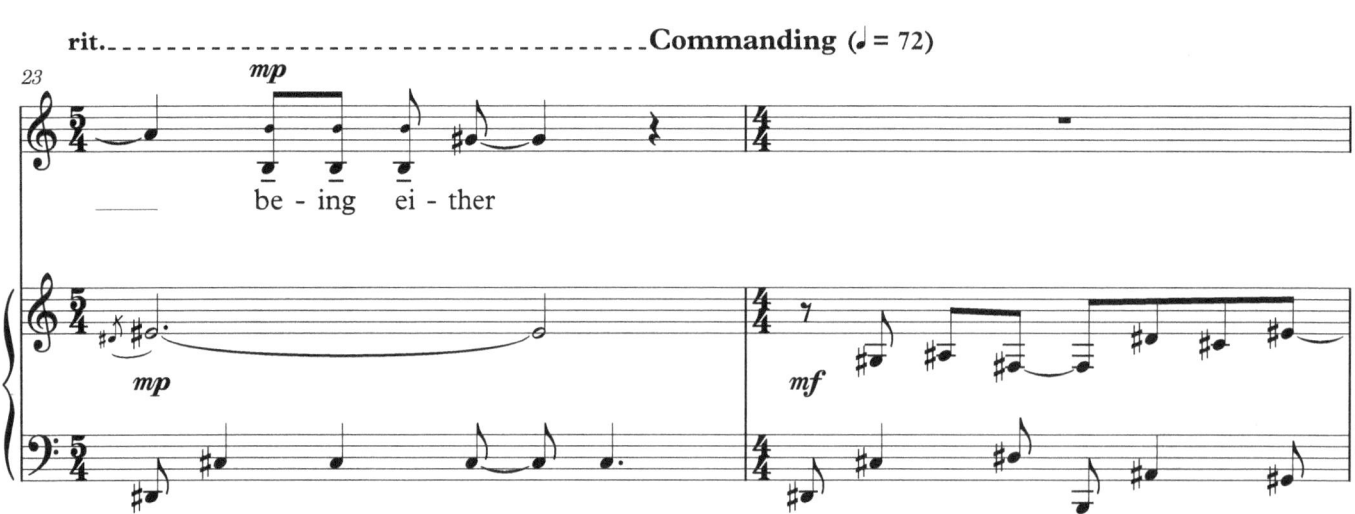

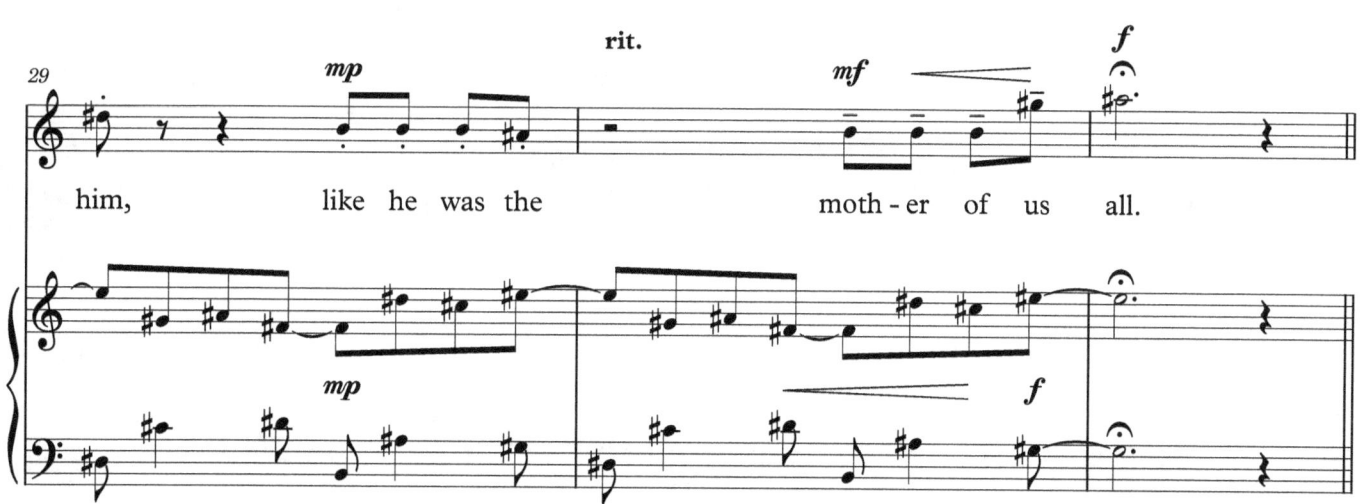

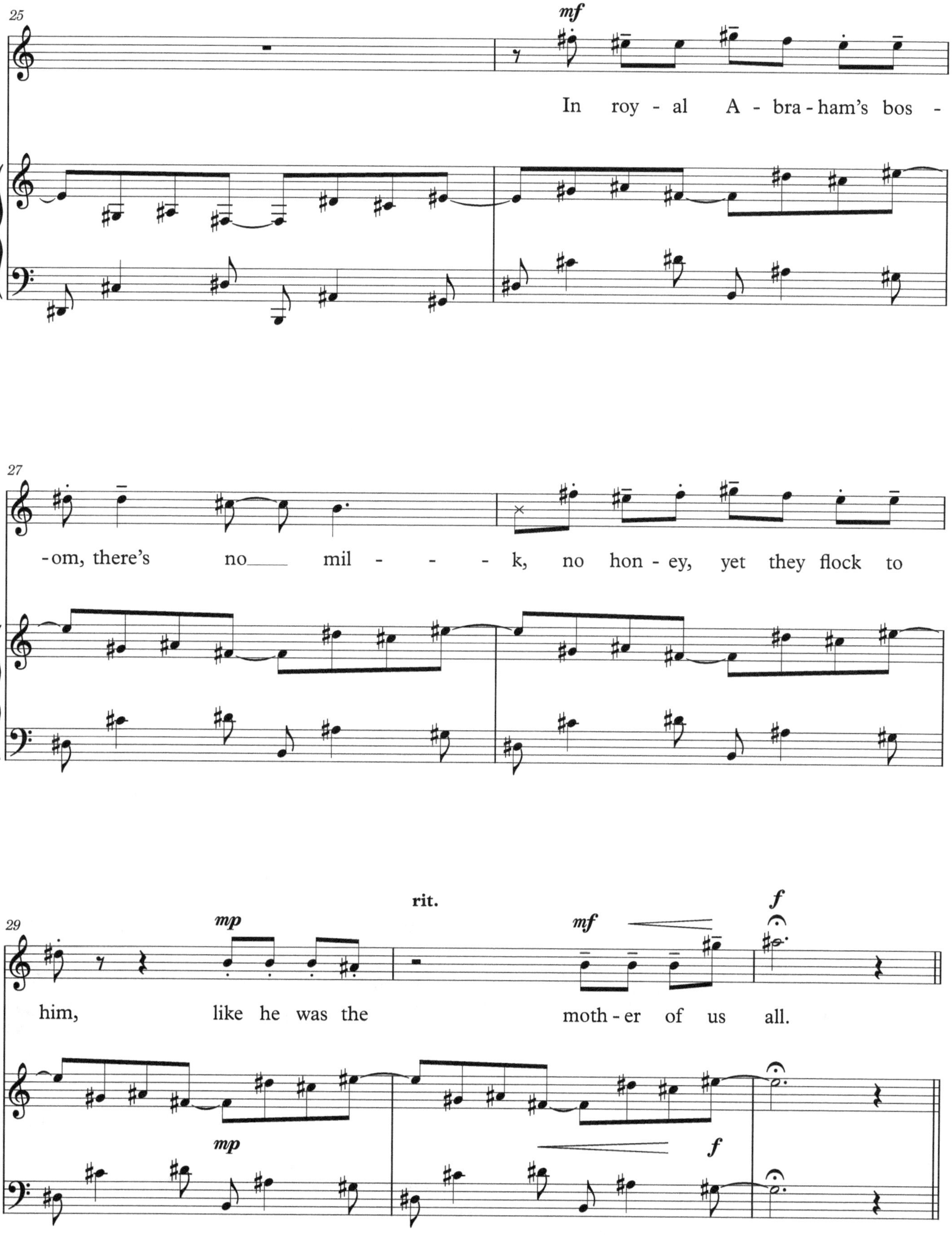

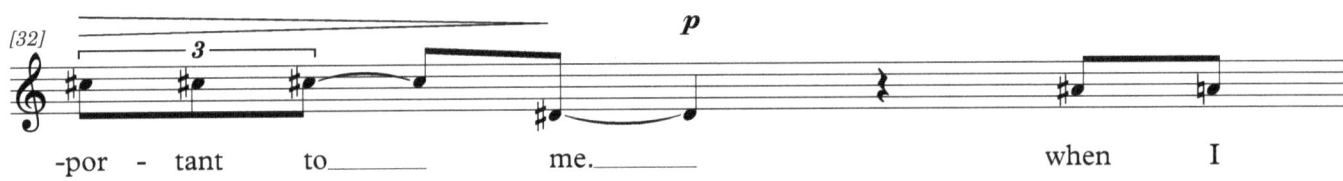

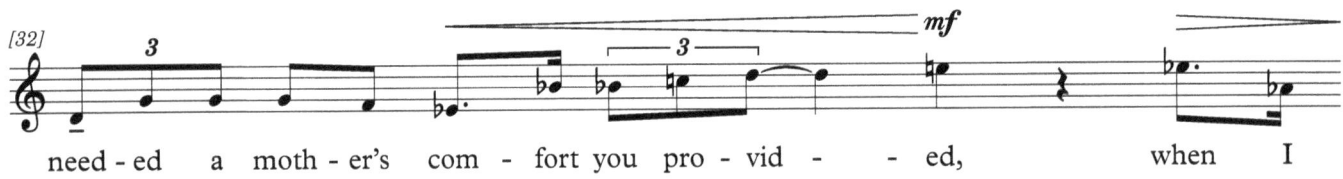

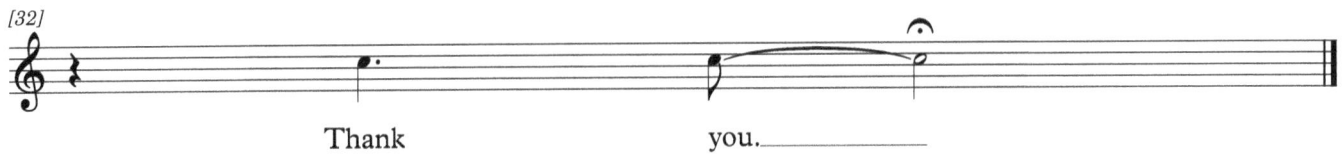

Commissioned by and dedicated to Sydney Bryant
Look Down Fair Moon

WALT WHITMAN

ALAN THEISEN
(2017)

Copyright © 2017 Alan Theisen. All Rights Reserved.

94

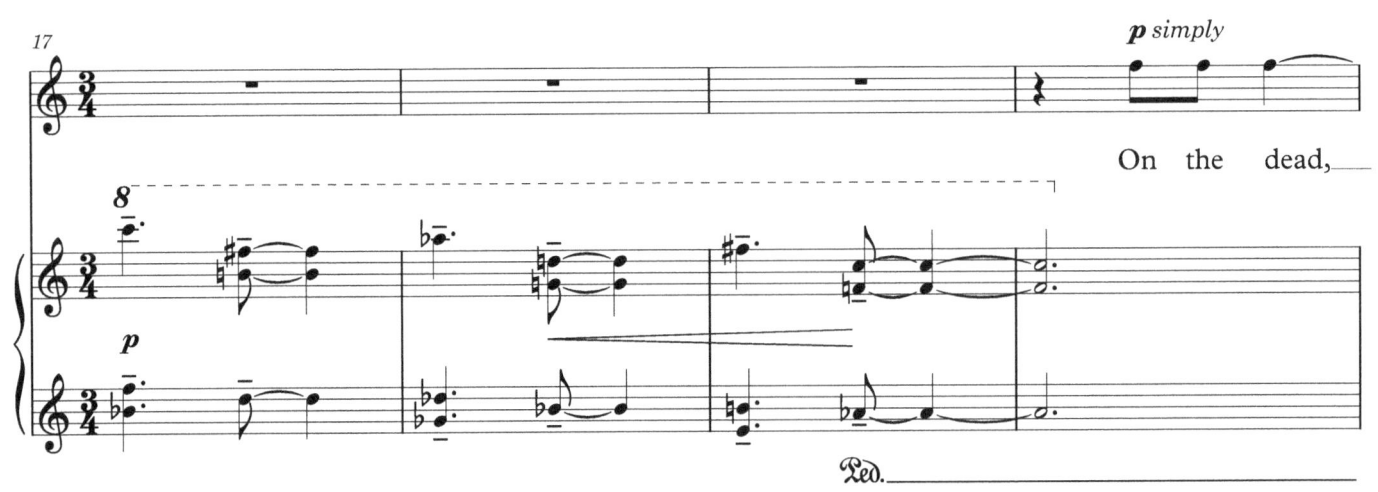

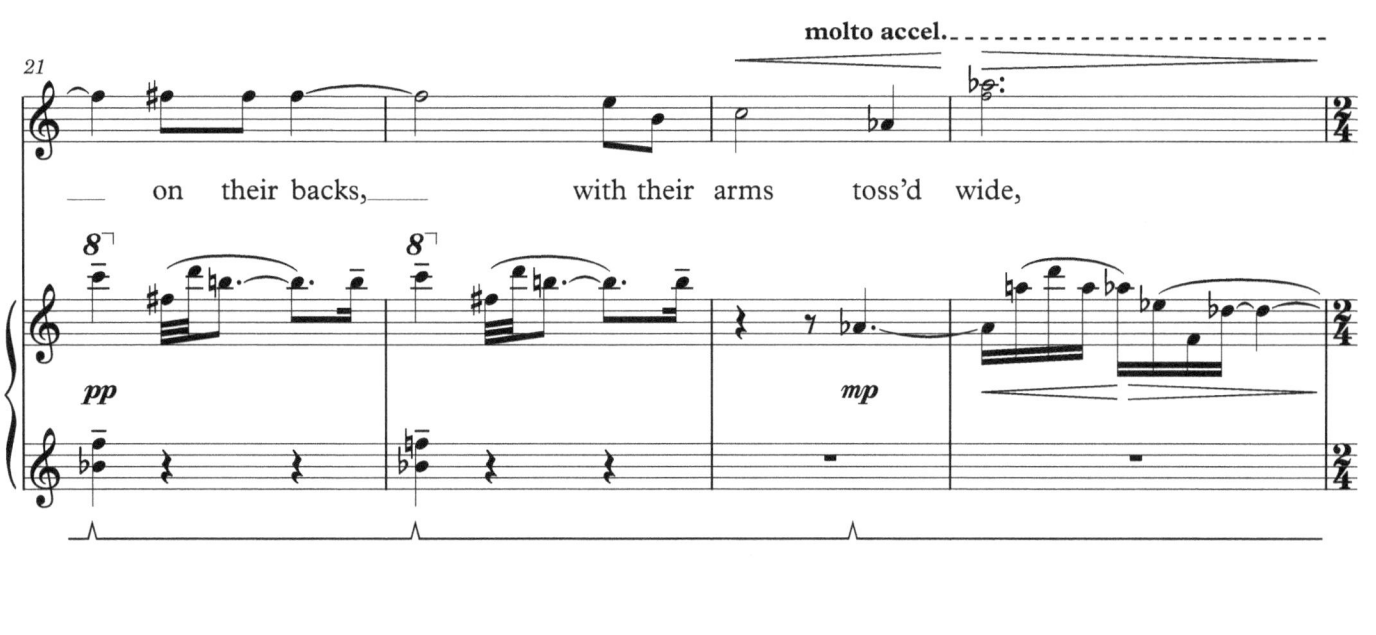
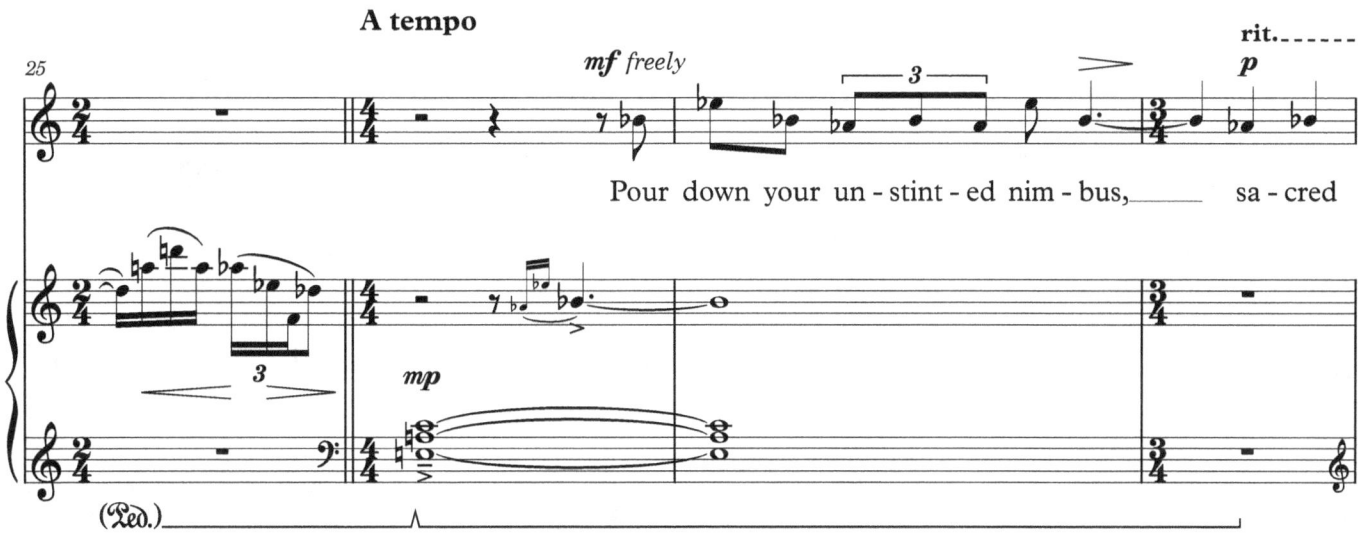
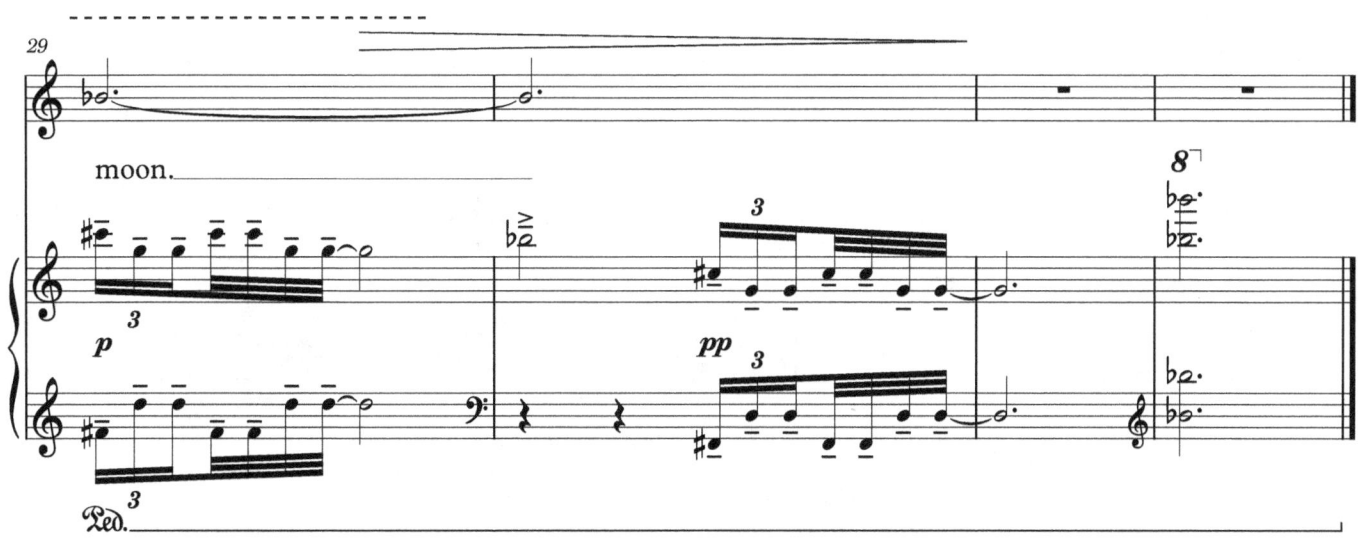

for Megan Ihnen
Good Bones

MAGGIE SMITH

DENNIS TOBENSKI
(2017)

Copyright © 2017 by Dennis Tobenski. All Rights Reserved.
"Good Bones" from *Weep Up,* Copyright © 2017 by Maggie Smith. Published by Tupelo Press.
Used with the kind permission of the author.

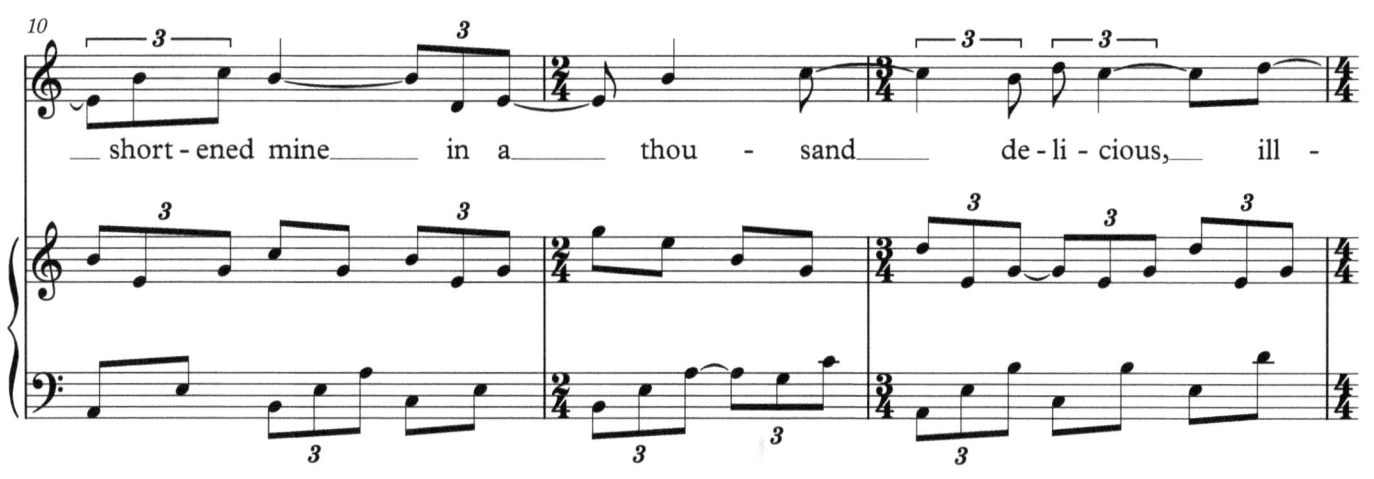

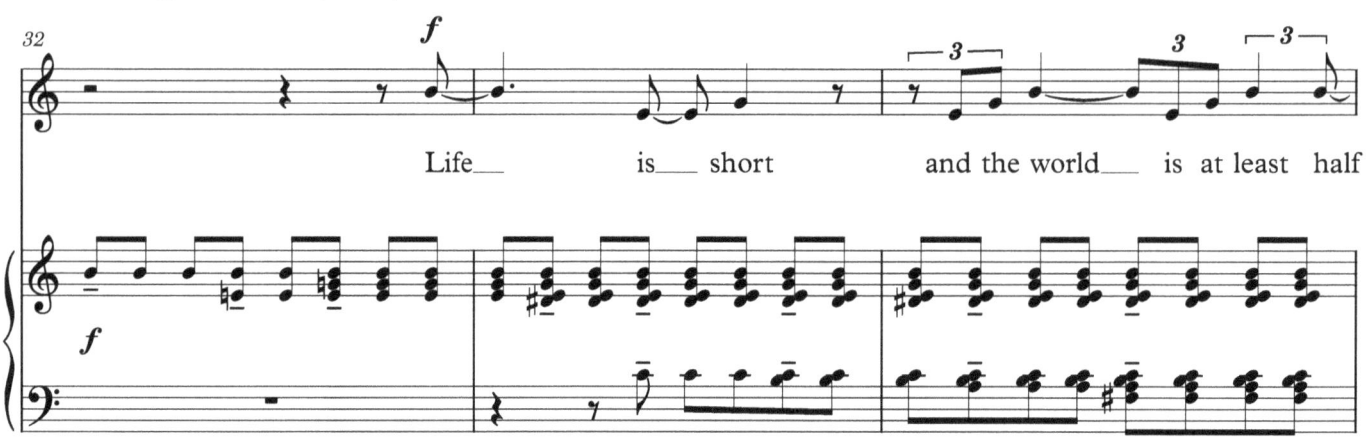

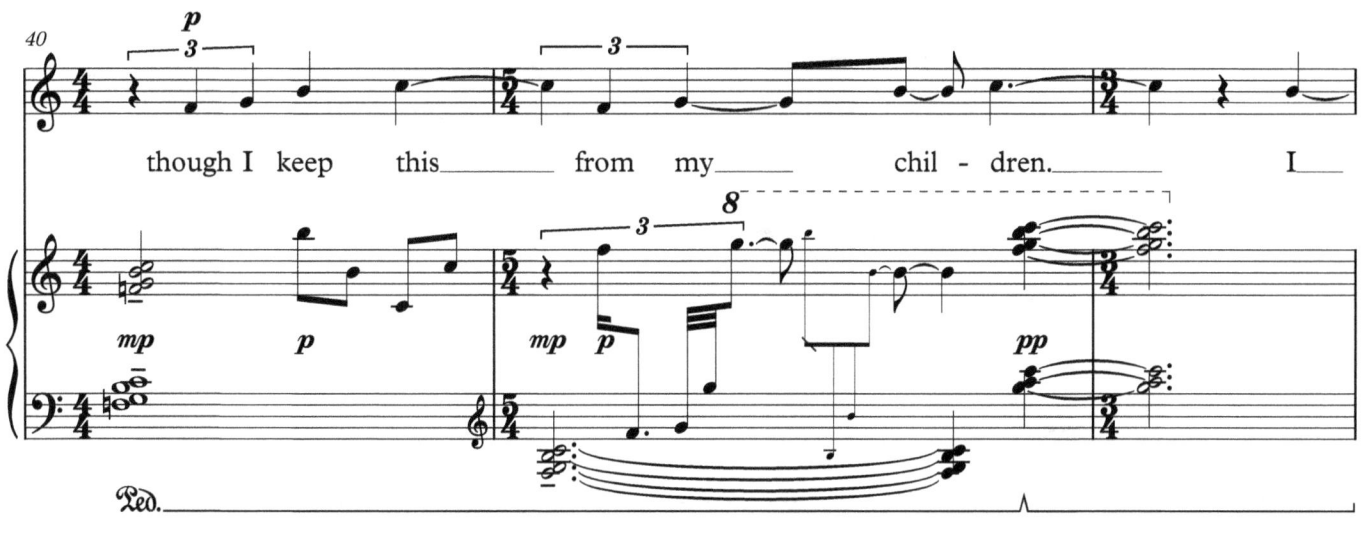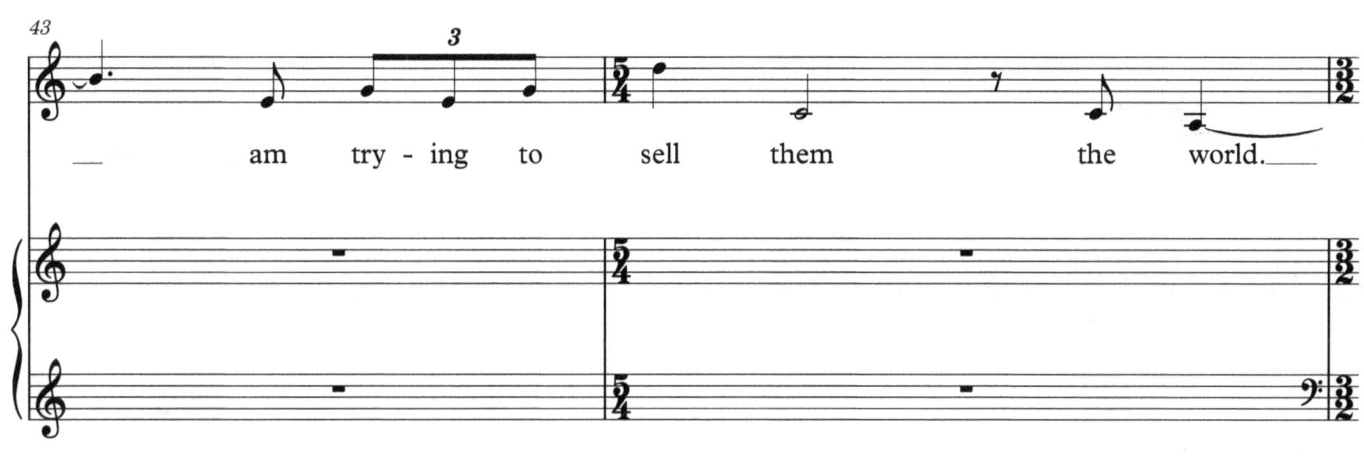

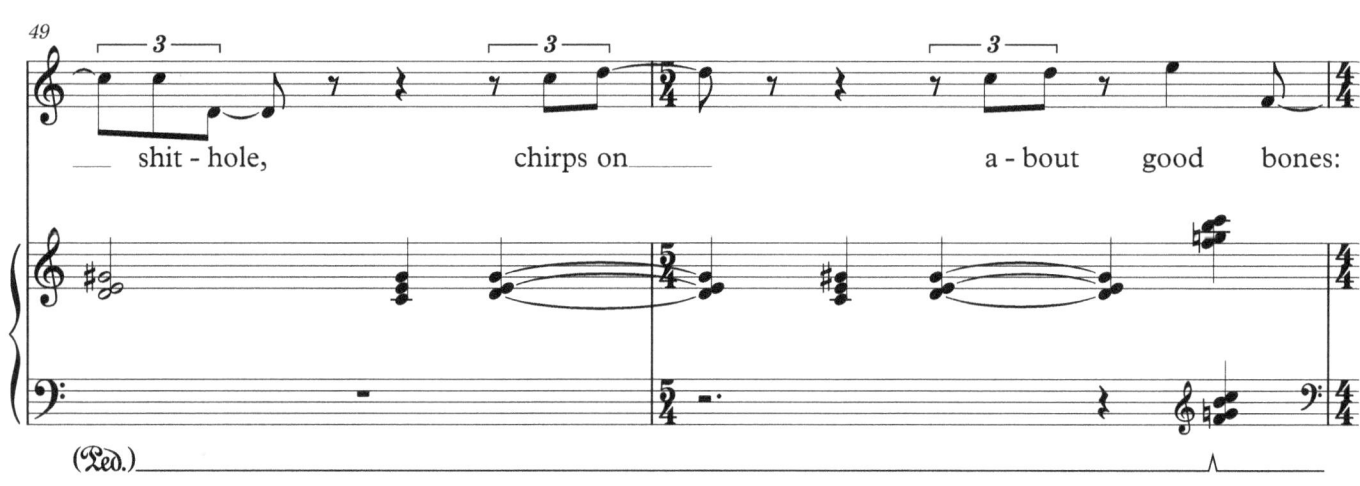
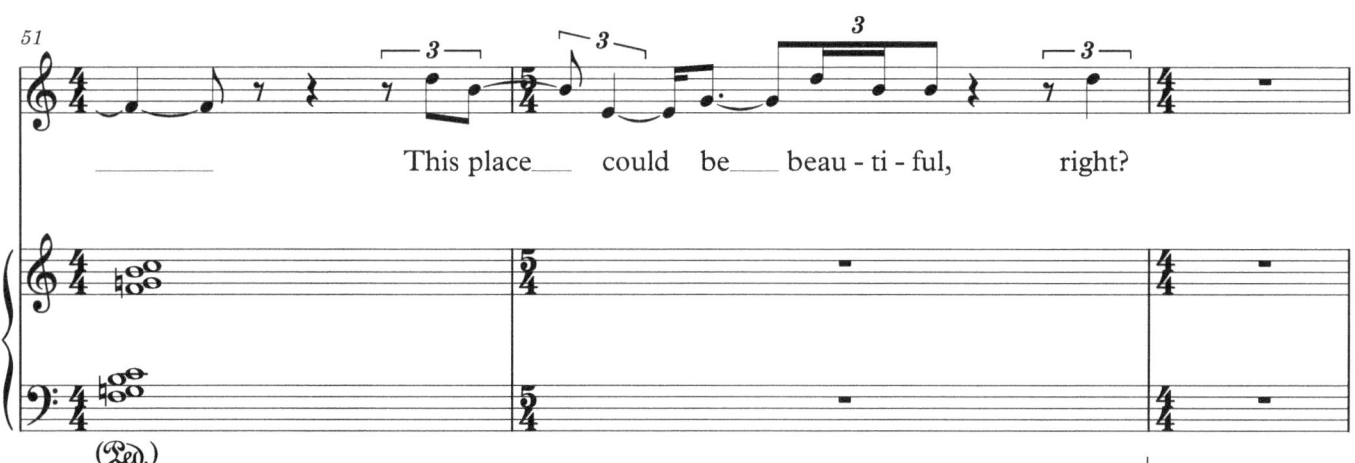

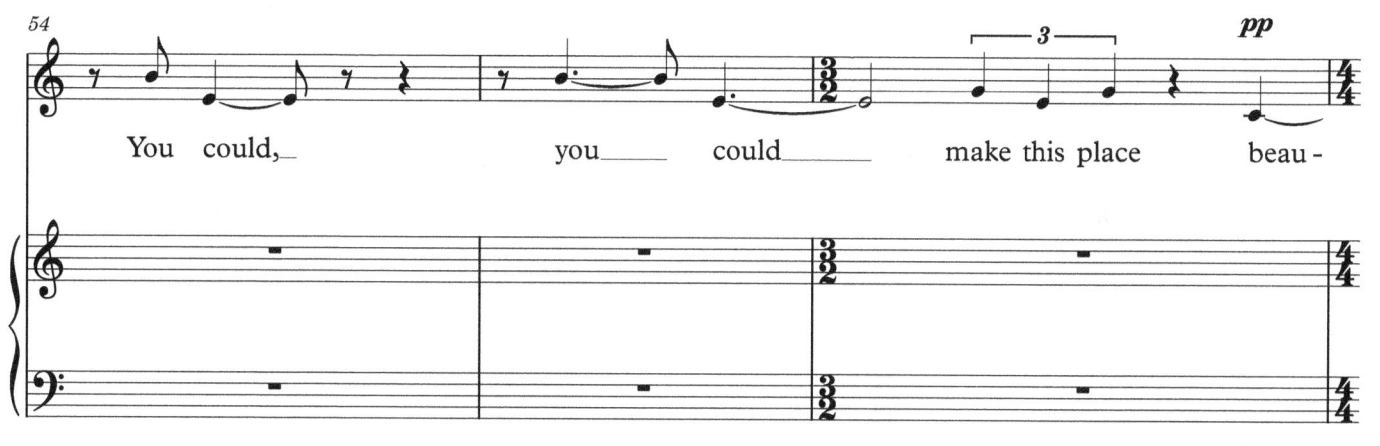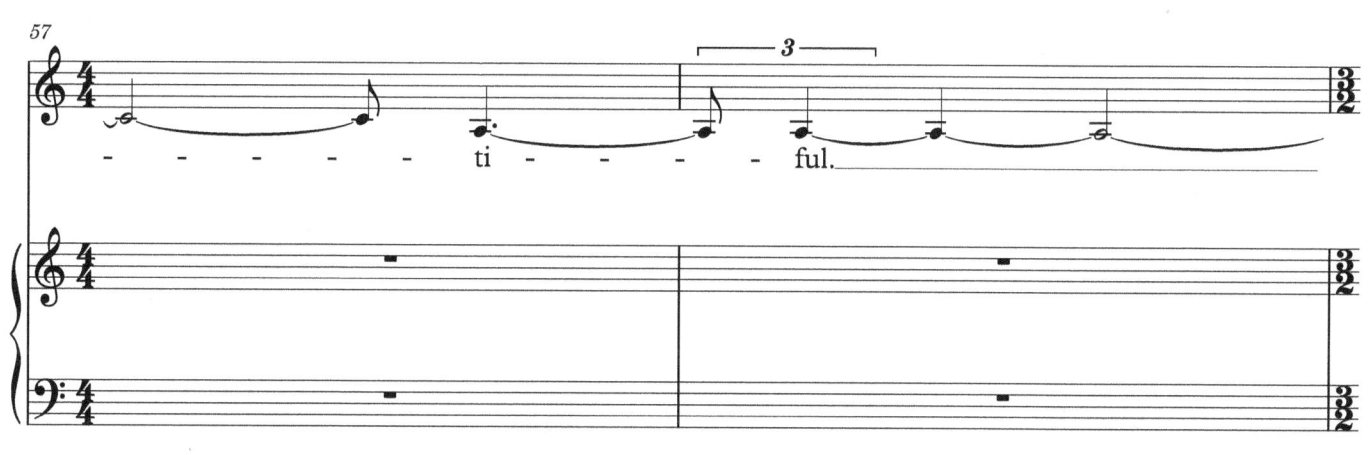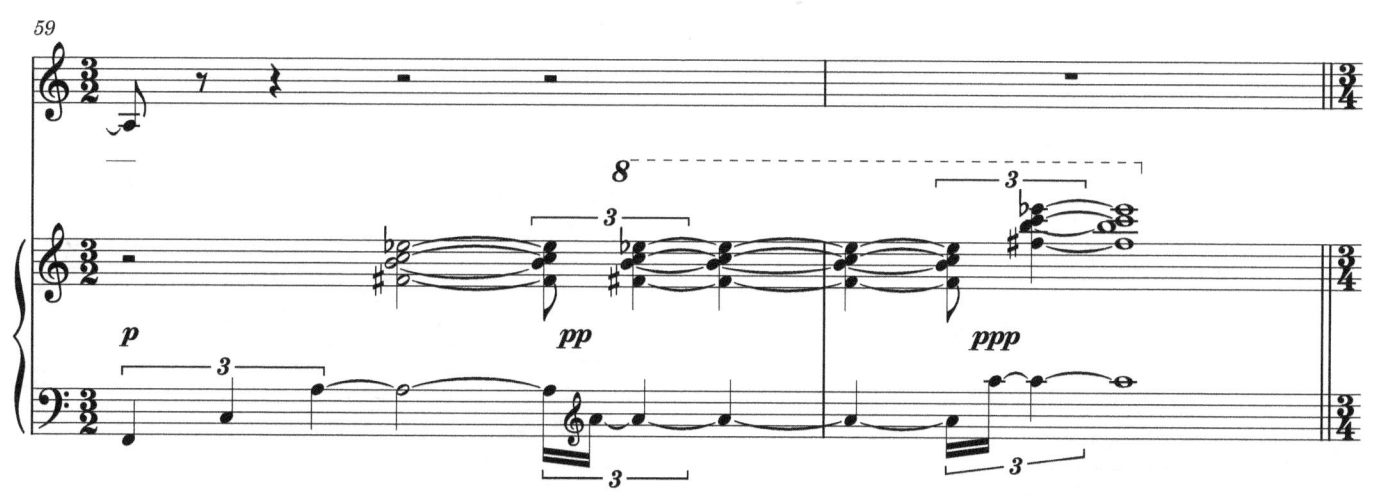

104

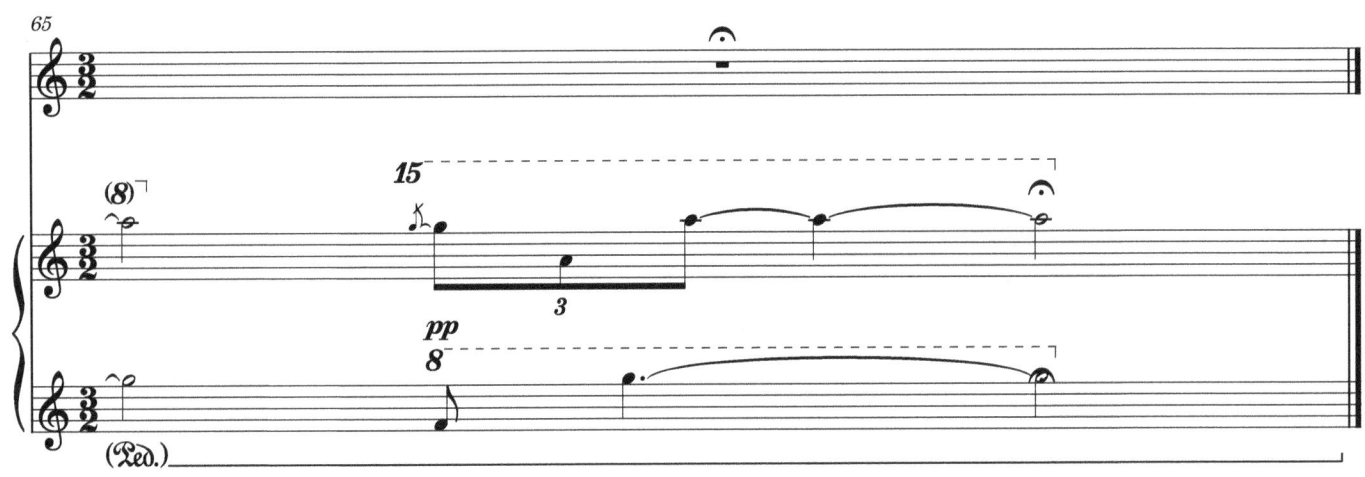

Dark Pines Under Water

GWENDOLYN MACEWEN

MOE TOUIZRAR
(2003)

"Dark Pines Under Water", from *The Shadow Maker*, by Gwendolyn MacEwen
Toronto: MacMillan of Canada, 1969, p.50. Text used by permission of the author's estate.
Music Copyright © 2003 by Moe Touizrar

108

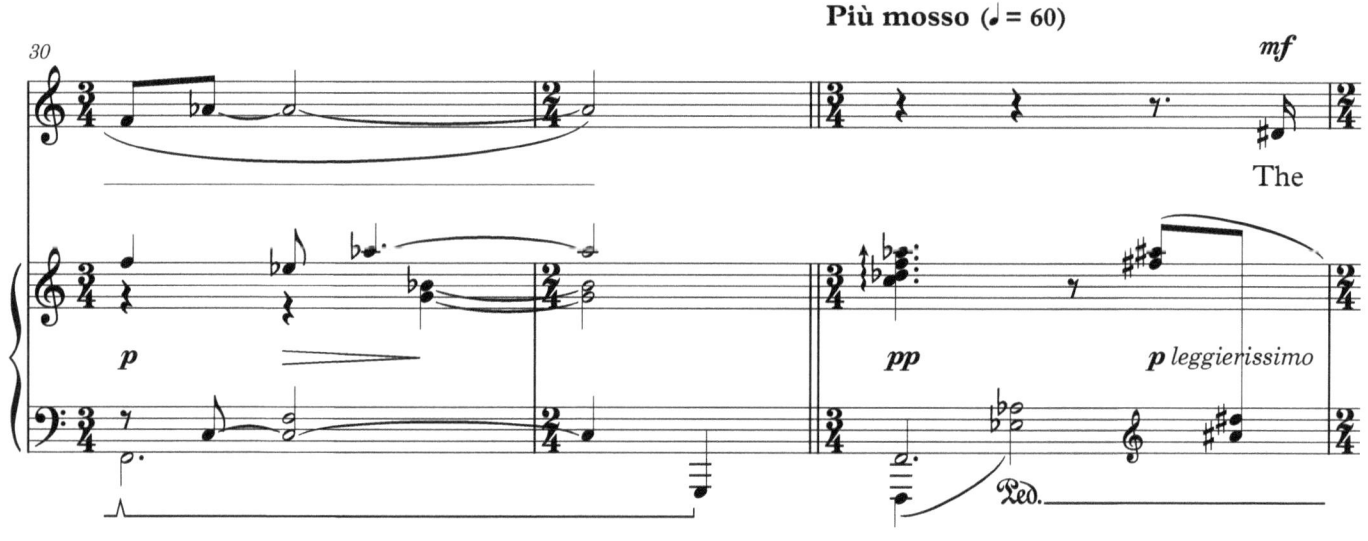
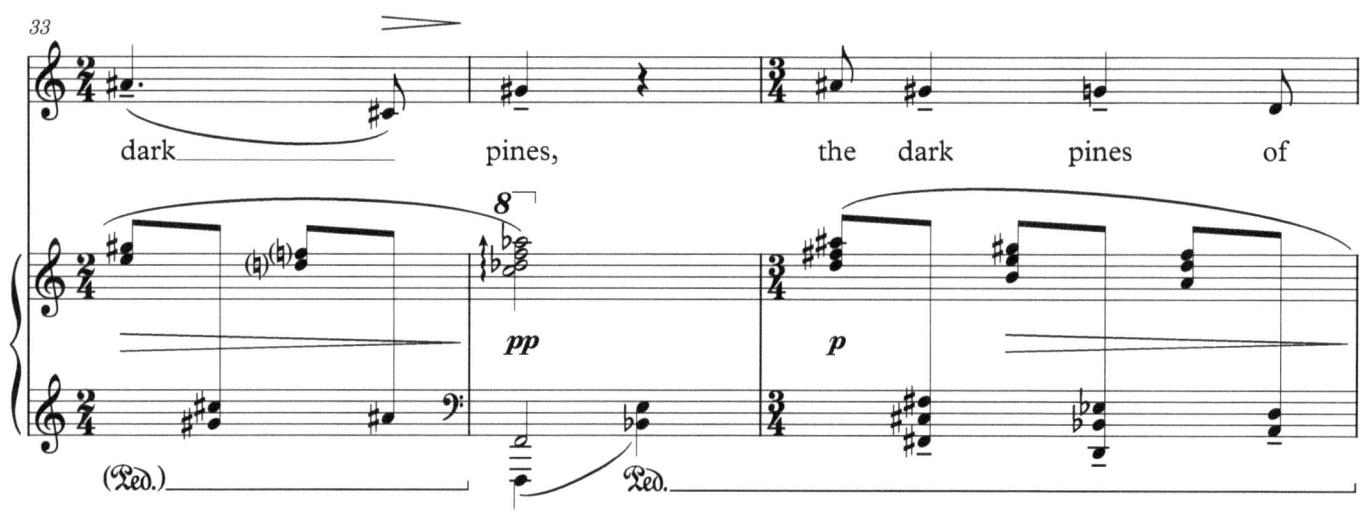

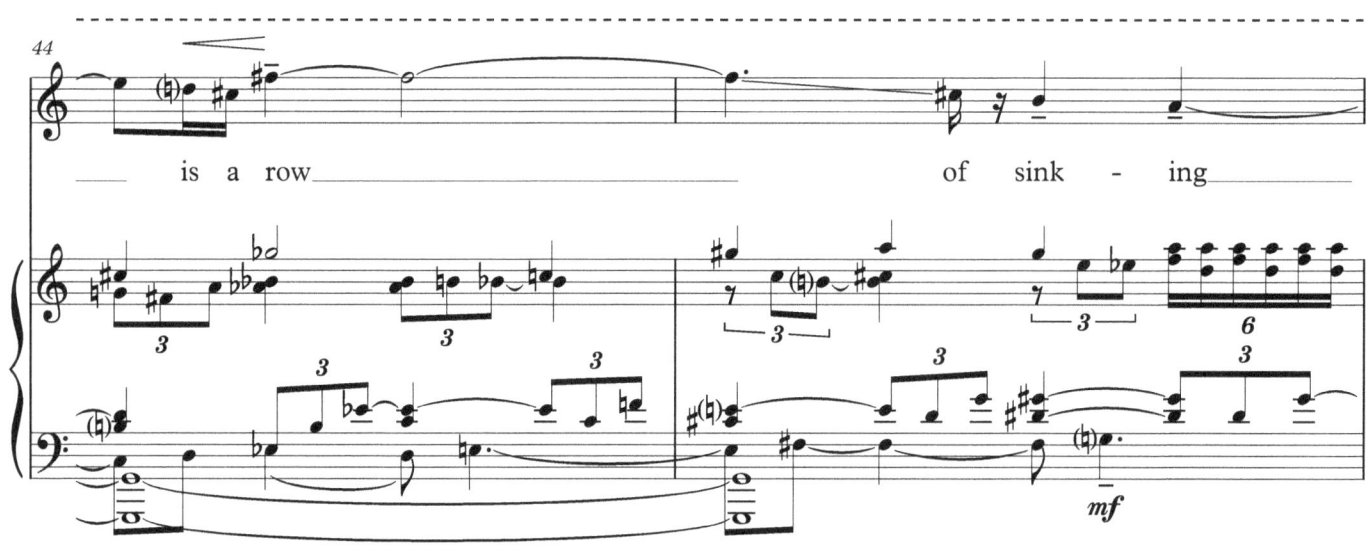

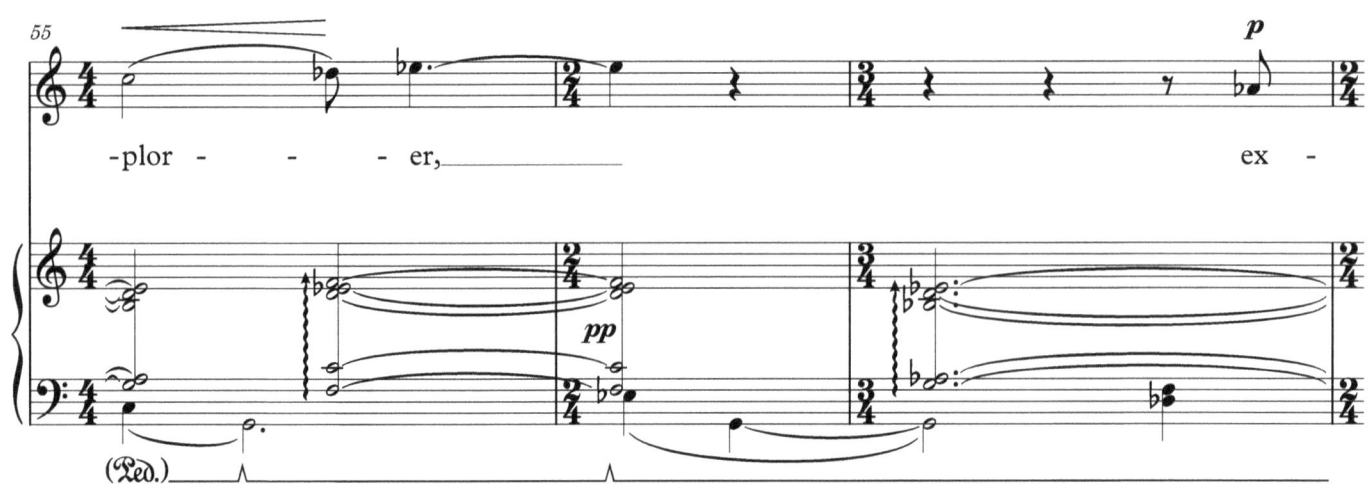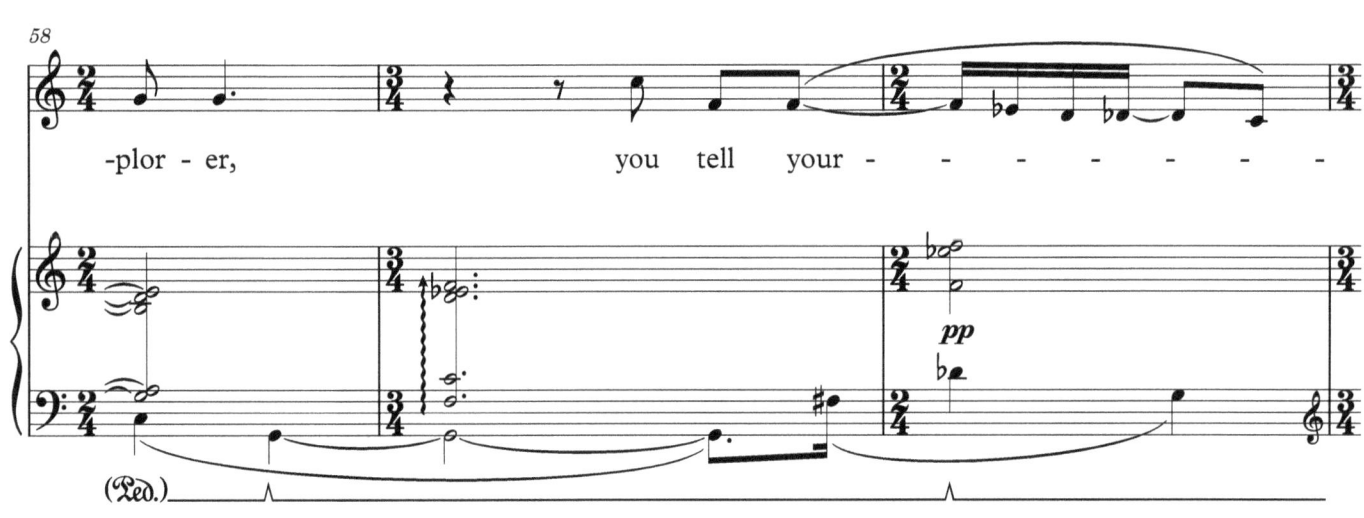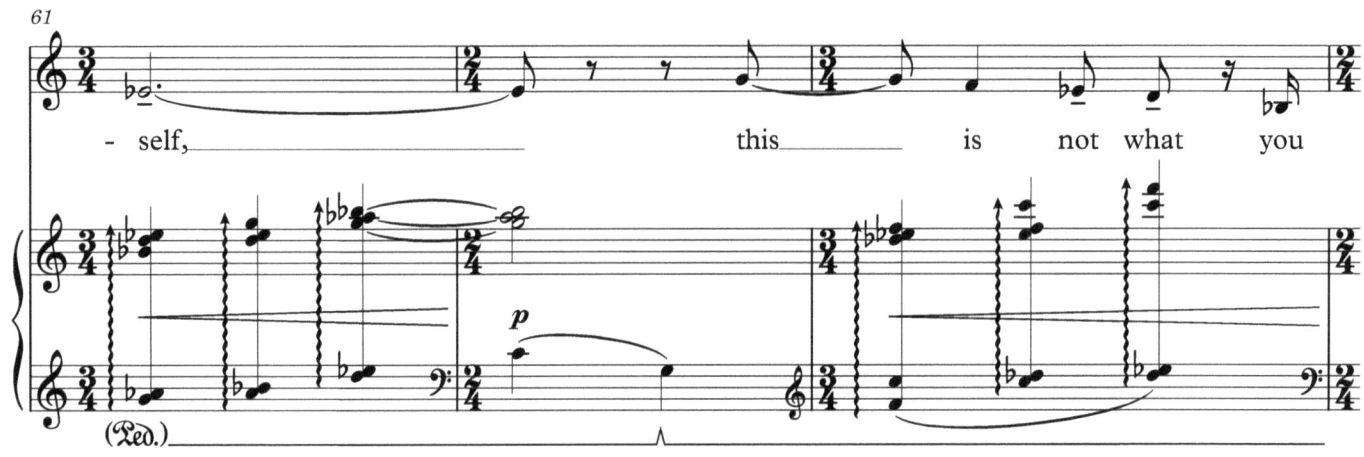

114

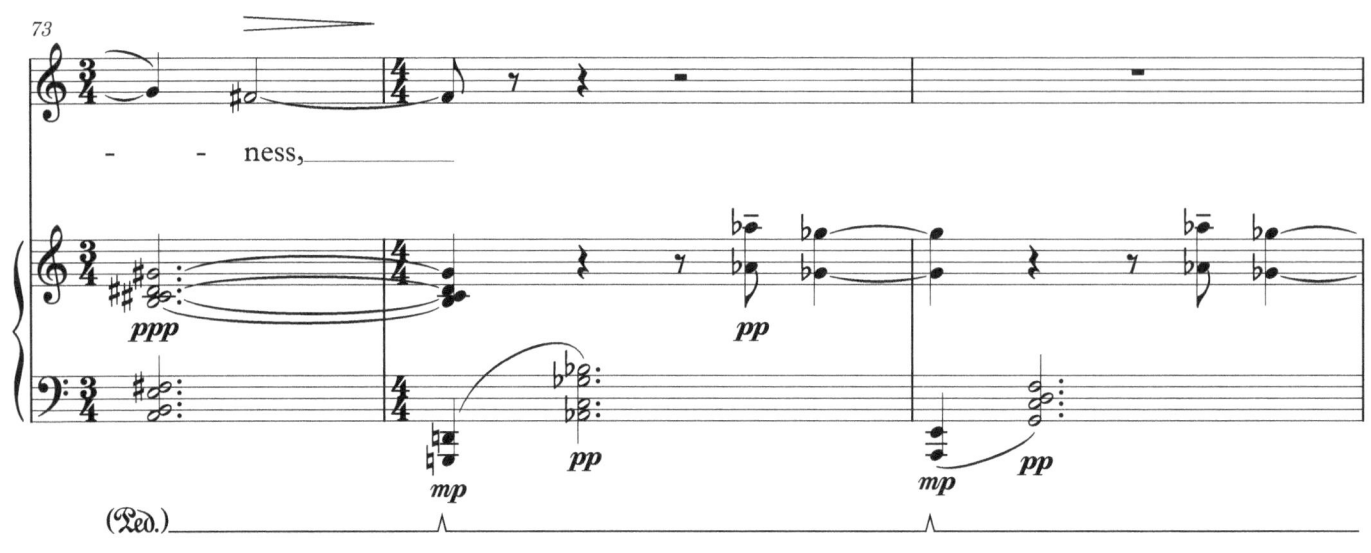

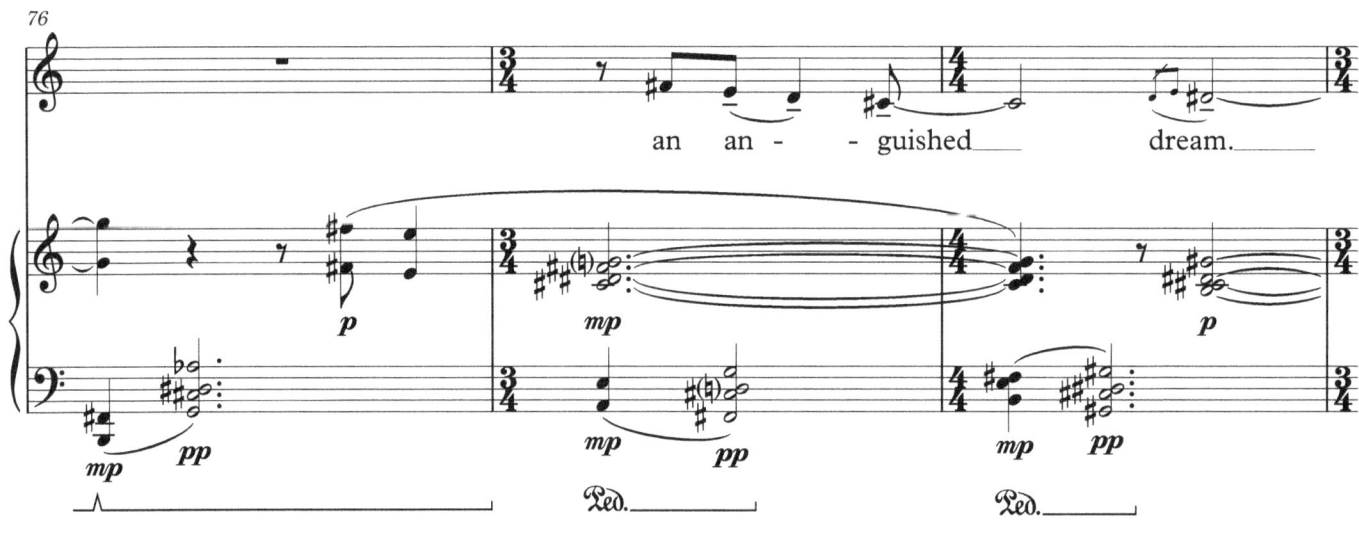

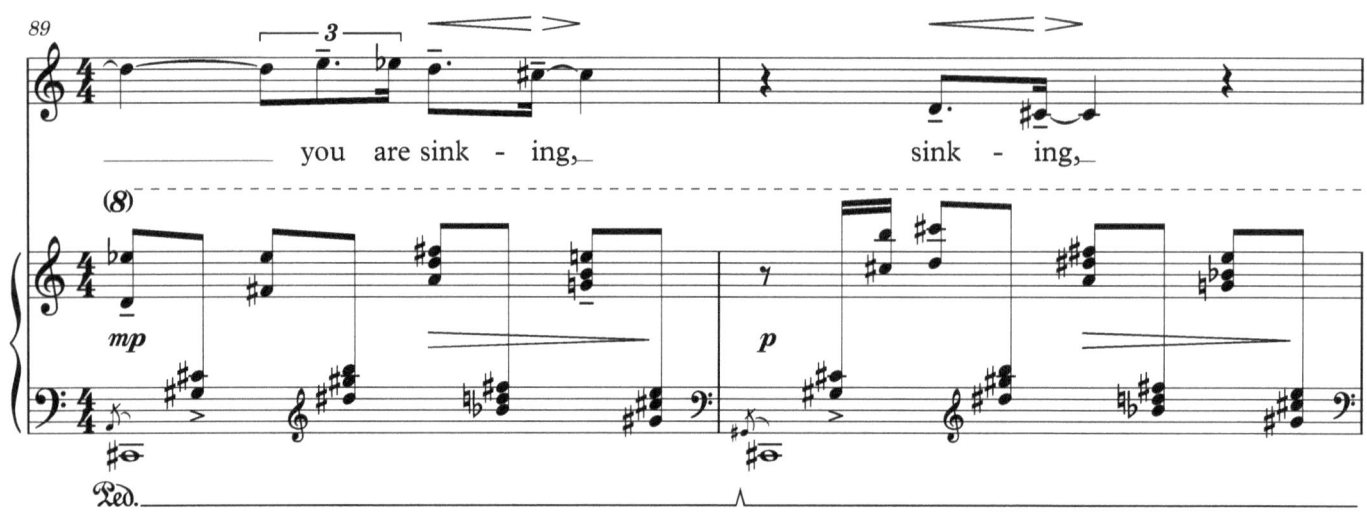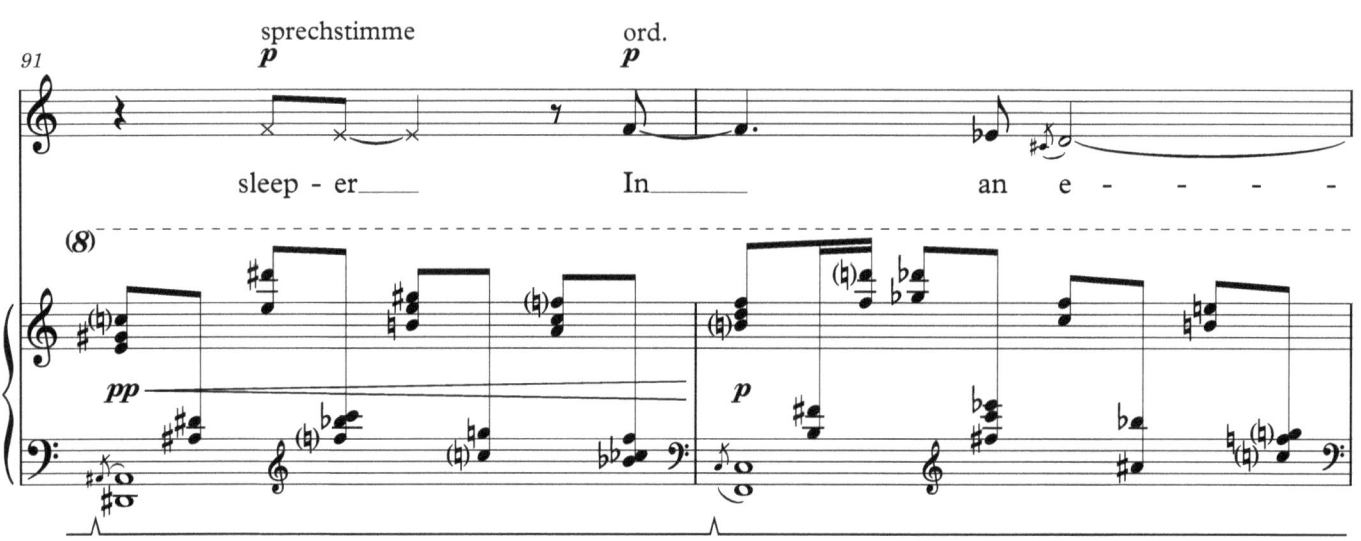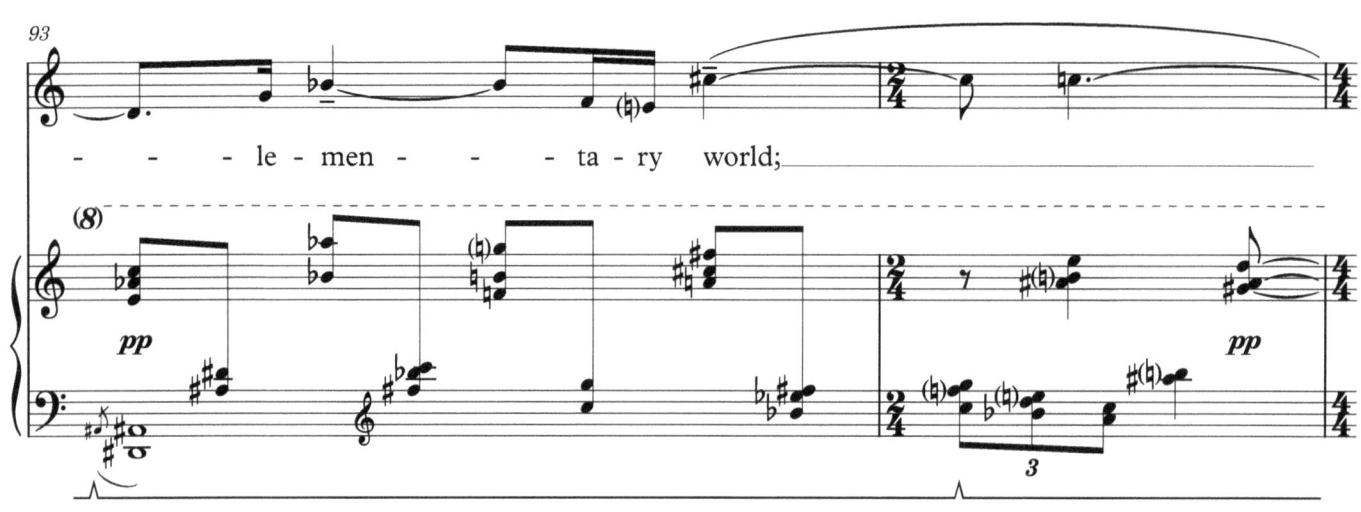

poco tratt.   a tempo

there

f

ff

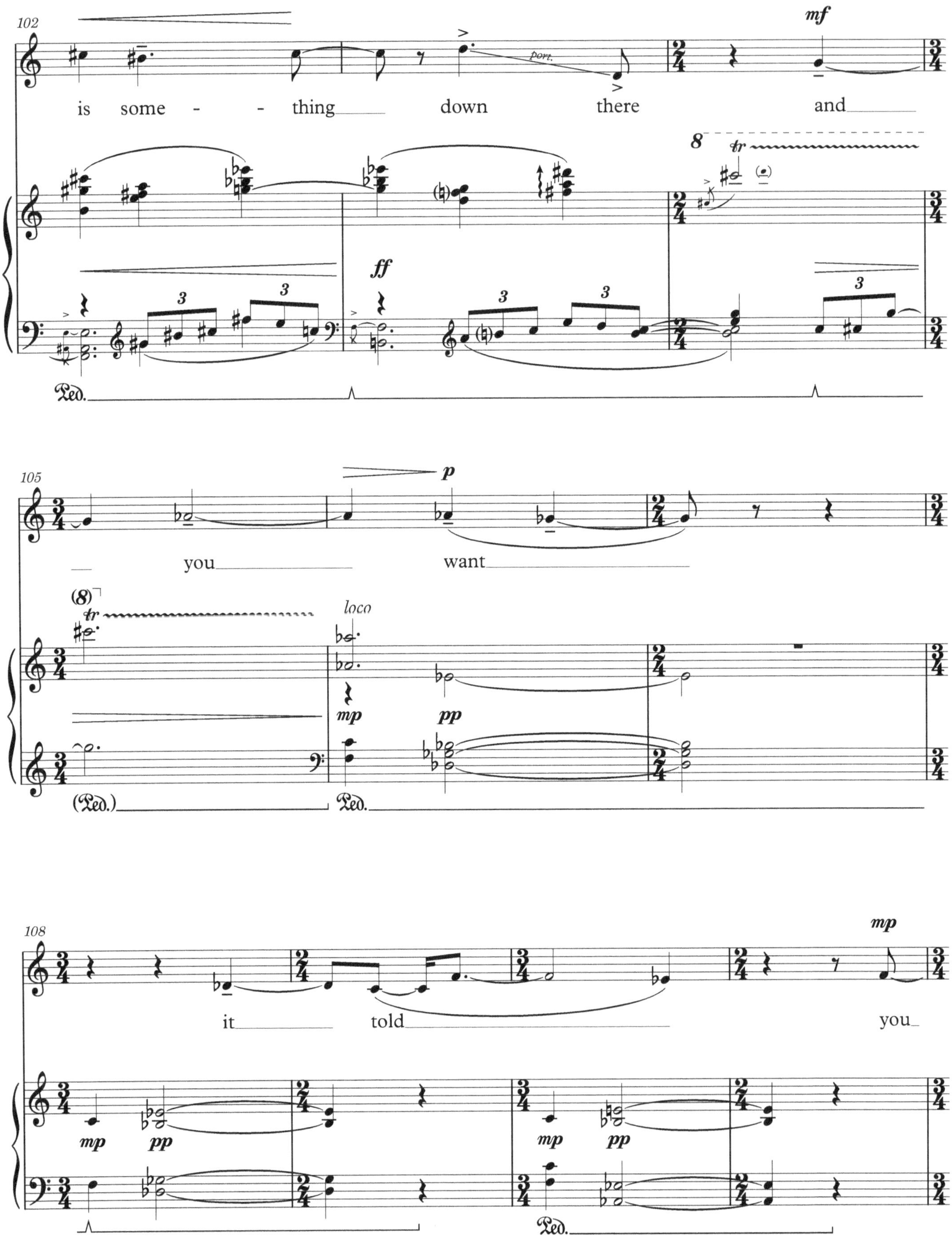

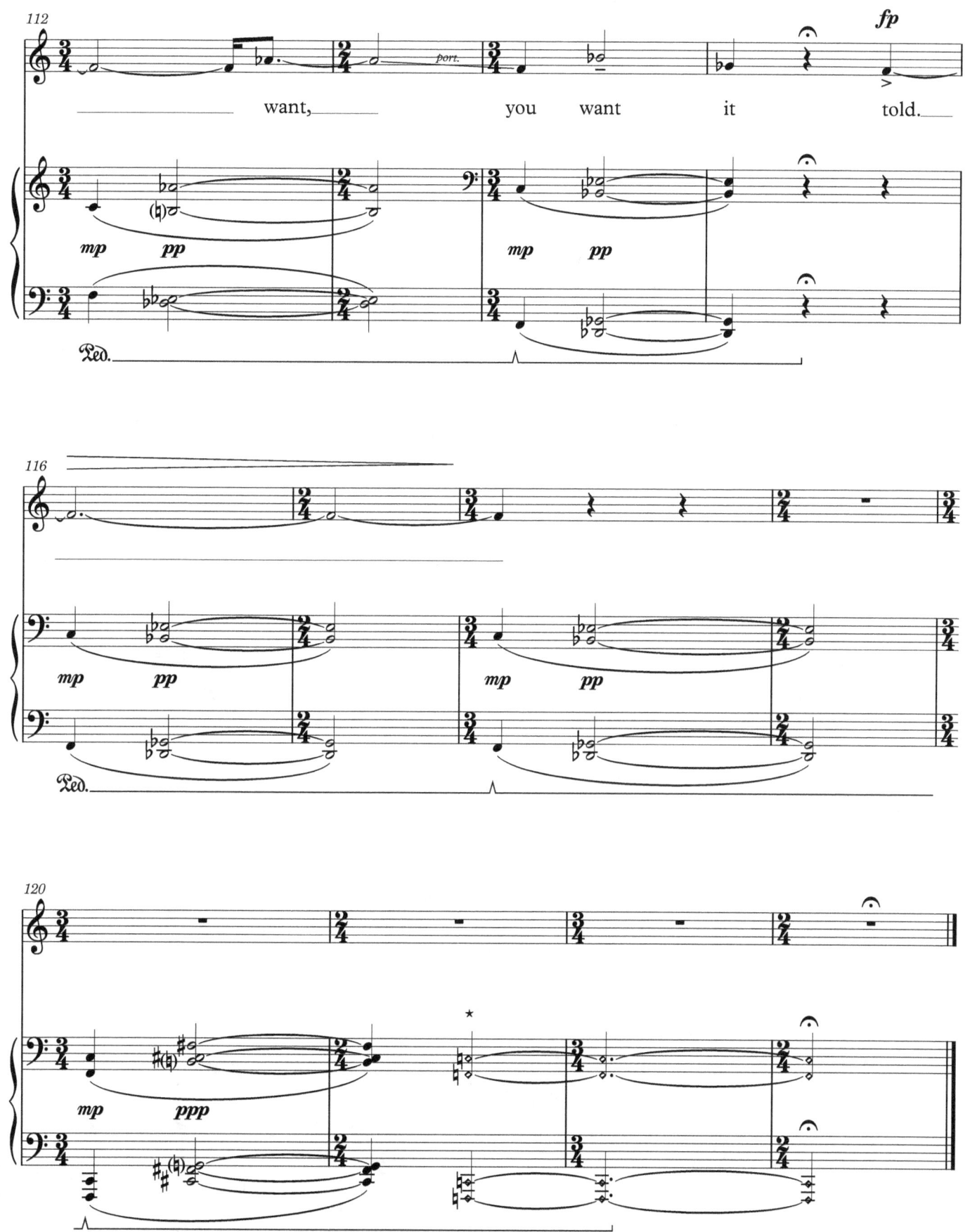

* depress keys silently and hold while releasing the pedal

Written for and dedicated to Anna Tonna

Blackbird Etude
from *Opus 22 Songs*

A.E. STALLINGS

ED WINDELS
(2013)

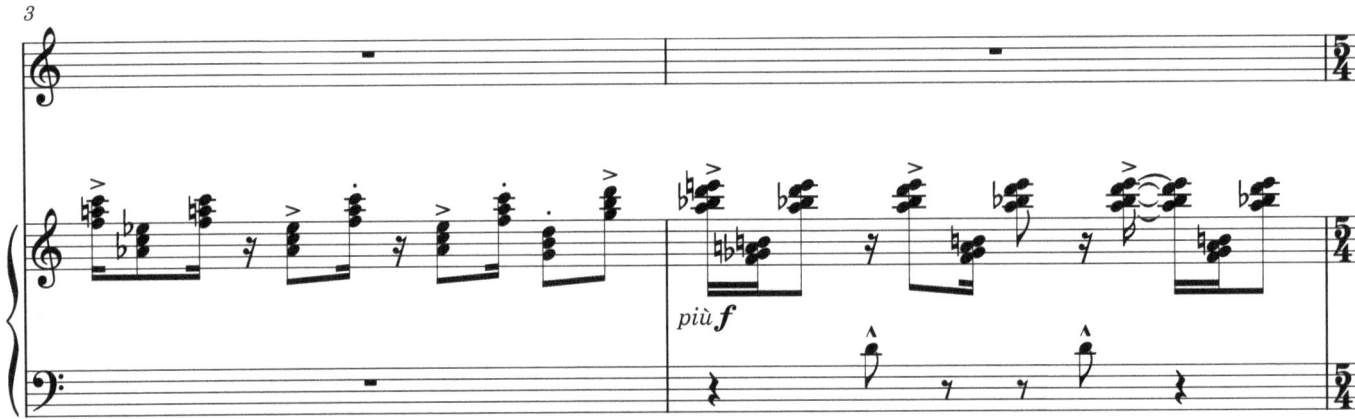

"Blackbird Etude" from *Olives: Poems* by A.E. Stallings, published by Evanston: TriQuarterly Books/Northwestern University Press, 2012. Used by permission of the author.

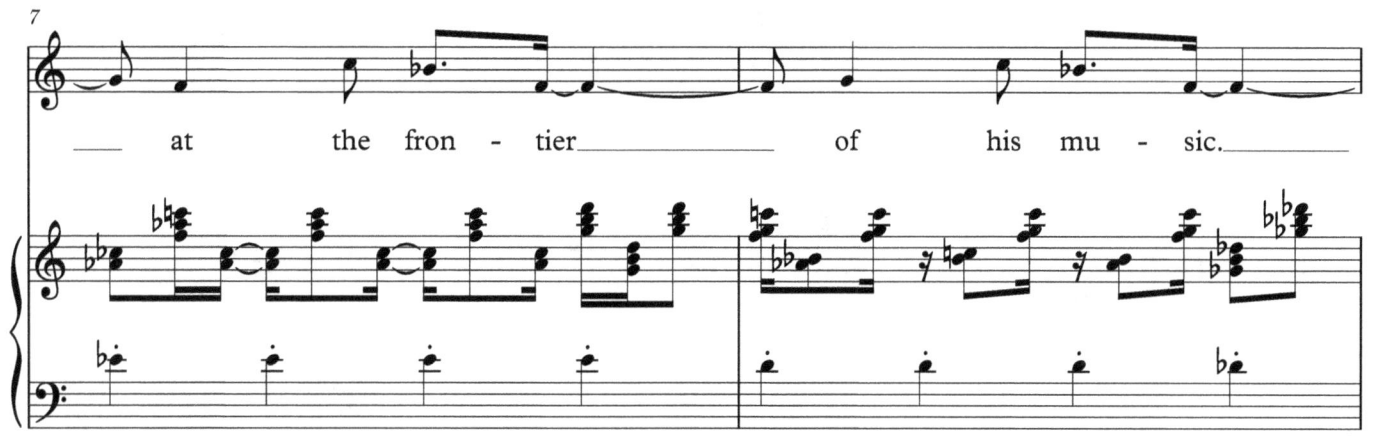

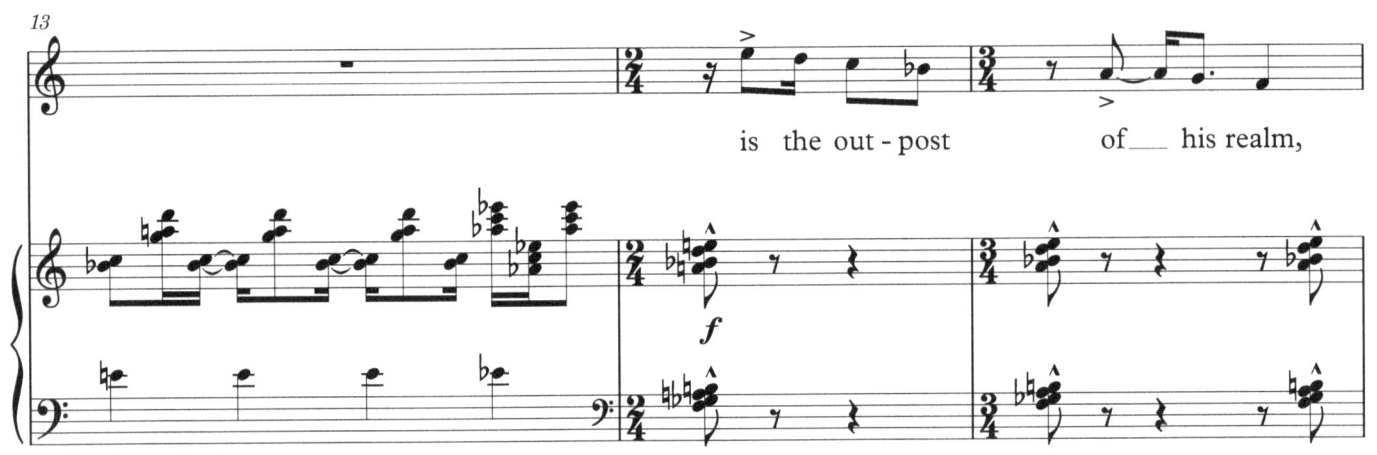

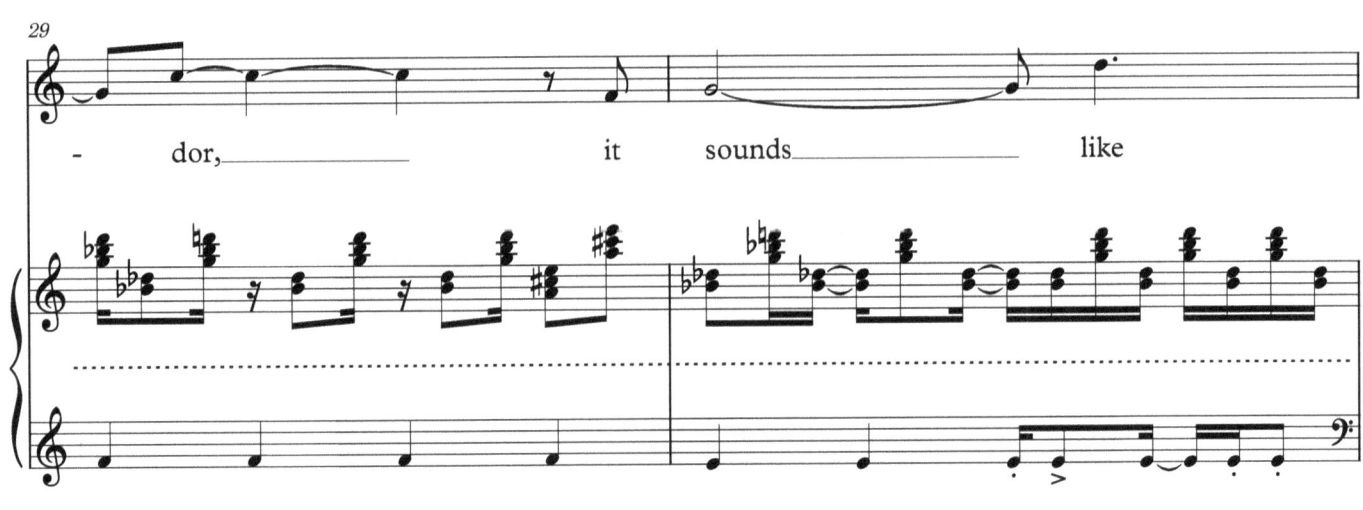

About the Curator
Megan Ihnen

www.meganihnen.com

American mezzo-soprano Megan Ihnen is recognized for her colorfully rich tone, powerful performance skills, and insightful musicianship in a diverse repertoire ranging from traditional works to the modern sounds of Crumb, Schwantner, Cage, and the most up-and-coming composers of her generation. Megan is a new music force of nature.

Ms. Ihnen is a founding member of the Seen/Heard Trio, whose model is dedicated to excellence and creativity in teaching and learning, immersive performance, audience experience, and developing the repertoire for the instrumentation of flute, harp, and voice. As musicians and recording artists, Seen/Heard Trio is devoted to featuring rarely-recorded or never-recorded composers.

A prolific new music artist, Ihnen's interpretations of modern and contemporary repertoire have garnered growing acclaim. She is particularly recognized as an excellent recitalist. Her *This World of Yes* program of contemporary music for voice and saxophone with Alan Theisen explores the themes of pathways, choices, and duality through the work of contemporary composers, and has been performed across the United States. Her program *Single Words She Once Loved* is a performance that centers around the ideas and effects of memory, dementia, and time. It is a deeply personal exploration of the dueling forces of 'eternal sunshine of the spotless mind' and 'God gave us memories so that we may have roses in winter'.

Ihnen was honored to receive a Phyllis Bryn-Julson Award for Commitment to and Performance of 20th/21st Century Music in 2009, and a Maryland State Arts Council Individual Artist Award in Classical Music: Solo Performance in 2014. She was an accomplished violist and drama student before pursuing degrees in music and vocal performance from Augustana University and the Peabody Institute of Johns Hopkins University.

In addition to being a avid podcast listener, Ihnen enjoys drinking good coffee, joking around with her sisters, tweeting about contemporary poetry, and watching Law & Order. She has grand dreams that one day her dog, Hunter, will be the best dog in the neighborhood. She lives in Des Moines, IA and out of her suitcase equally.

About the Composers

Michael Betteridge (PRS)

b. 1988

michaelbetteridge@hotmail.com
www.michaelbetteridge.com

Betteridge is a composer from Manchester, UK with an interest in creating work that challenges and inspires audiences and performers alike.

His work has been performed by and commissioned by London Symphony Orchestra, Birmingham Contemporary Music Group, soprano Sarah Leonard, violinist Nicola Benedetti, amongst others, as well as having been performed on BBC Radio 3 and 4.

Recent large works include: the Anglo-Icelandic Twitter opera *#echochamber* that premiered in Reykjavik in May 2018 before embarking on a UK tour; a 15 minute collection of new choral songs for male voices and piano with words by poet Andrew McMillan; and a 50 minute song cycle for young voices titled *Do you see? Do your hear?* commissioned by Birmingham Contemporary Music Group (BCMG) alongside the Royal Society of the Arts.

Twitter: @mbetteridge

Mark Buller (ASCAP)

b. 1986

mark@markbullercomposer.com
www.markbullercomposer.com

The music of composer and pianist Mark Buller has been performed around the country and internationally, from Carnegie Hall and the Menil Collection to various venues on five continents. He has been commissioned by a wide range of organizations, including the Atlanta Symphony Orchestra, Houston Grand Opera (for two 45-minute operas, an extended choral work, and numerous art songs), the Houston Symphony, Da Camera of Houston, and River Oaks Chamber Orchestra.

Winner of the Rapido! Composition Contest, the Vanguard Voices Choral Composition Competition, and the Sarofim Composition Award, his recent performances include "Motion Studies" by Boston Musica Viva, Voices of Change (Dallas), Atlanta Chamber Players, and Detroit Chamber Winds & Strings; "The Songs of Ophelia" by the Atlanta Symphony Orchestra and director Robert Spano; and "Overboard," a 10-minute choral work with text by Leah Lax, commissioned by Houston Grand Opera. Upcoming performances include a third commissioned work for River Oaks Chamber Orchestra, an English horn concerto for Brett Linski, a song cycle for mezzo-soprano Abigail Levis, and a left hand-only work for pianist Geraldine Ong.

Facebook: www.facebook.com/markbullercomposer

Stephen DeCesare (BMI)

b. 1969

www.sdecesare.com

DeCesare, as a composer, is an autodidact. He has over 1200 compositions in his catalog which include religious songs, a Requiem Mass, orchestral pieces, and musicals. He has enjoyed national and international success with many of his compositions such as the "Our Lady of Fatima" and "A Christmas Carol" musicals, which after they had appeared in Providence R.I. have had many performances in theatres across the U.S.A and Europe.

In 2011, Stephen musically directed and premiered his "Mass of Divine Mercy" at the beatification of Pope John Paul II which aired live on EWTN at the National Shrine of Divine Mercy in Stockbridge, MA

Douglas Fisk (ASCAP)

b. 1976

contact@douglasfiskmusic.com
www.douglasfiskmusic.com

Douglas Fisk is active as a composer, pianist, and teacher. His music has been performed by artists including members of the New York New Music Ensemble, percussionist Gwendolyn Dease, baritone Malcolm Merriweather, and Sospiro Winds. He began compositional studies with Paul Barsom and Bruce Trinkley at the Pennsylvania State University before studying with Martin Bresnick and Ezra Laderman at the Yale School of Music. He has attended the Oregon Bach Festival Composers Symposium, the June in Buffalo festival, the European American Musical Alliance program in Paris, France, where he studied with Claude Baker, and been in residence at the Millay Colony for the Arts. He's presented his music in master classes with Narcis Bonet, David Felder, Joel Hoffman, Bernard Rands, Augusta Reed Thomas, and Charles Wuorinen.

He is the co-director of the Composers/Pianists Concert Series, a series in which composer/pianists perform their own solo piano works and ensemble pieces with piano; concerts have been presented at Merkin Hall, Tenri Cultural Institute, the Longy School of Music, and Firehouse12.

His *Impromptu* for solo marimba appears on the Gwendolyn Dease (Burgett) recording: *Boomslang: New Music for Marimba*.

Matt Frey (BMI)

b. 1980

mattfreynyc@gmail.com
www.musicbymattfrey.com

The music of Brooklyn-based composer Matt Frey creates intimately sentimental sonic worlds inflected with churning rhythms, minimalist-like textures, and extended moments of restless tension.

Frey's vocal works—comprising song cycles, music-theater works, and opera—explore the interplay of text, drama, and music to make a palpable, instantaneous connection with an audience. Frey's vocal music has been performed and workshopped across the U.S. and in Canada at festivals and programs including Fort Worth Opera's Frontiers, the Crane School of Music, Opera From Scratch, the New Dramatists Composer-Librettist and PlayTime Development Studios, the John Duffy Composers Institute, and the BMI Lehman Engel Musical Theater Workshop.

His instrumental music explores a more abstract approach to narrative, focusing on the concept of tension and release. Often using harmonic or melodic inspiration from popular or electronic music to infuse his compositions, Frey's music has been commissioned and presented by ensembles such as the String Orchestra of Brooklyn, Synergy Percussion, the JACK String Quartet, the West Point Woodwind Quintet, the NYU Symphony Orchestra, Cadillac Moon Ensemble, Echo Chamber, andPlay, the Manhattan Wind Ensemble.

Frey is a graduate of the Masters program in Music Composition at New York University and holds an undergraduate degree in Music Composition from Brooklyn College, where he studied with composers including Jason Eckardt, Douglas Geers, Joan La Barbara, Tania León, Robert Maggio, and Julia Wolfe.

Jodi Goble (ASCAP)

b. 1974

www.jodigoble.com

Composer Jodi Goble writes text-based, character-driven music fueled by her extensive background as a vocal coach and song-specialist collaborative pianist. Her compositions are praised for their melodism, their intuitive, idiomatic vocal writing, and the clarity and deftness of their text settings, and have been performed across the United States and internationally and featured on National Public Radio. She is the 2013 winner of the Iowa Music Teachers Association Commission Competition and the 2017 runner-up in the National Association of Teachers of Singing Art Song Competition. She also placed as a NATS ASCA finalist in 2008 and as the honorable mention winner in 2016.

Until 2009, Goble was a member of the voice faculty at Boston University's College of Fine Arts, senior vocal coach and Coordinator of Opera Programs for the Boston University Tanglewood Institute, and primary rehearsal pianist of the Boston Symphony Orchestra's Tanglewood Festival Chorus, where she played under conductors James Levine, Bernard Haitink, Sir Colin Davis, Rafael Fruhbeck de Burgos, Keith Lockhart, John Oliver, and Seiji Ozawa, and collaborated in rehearsal with artists José van Dam, Paul Groves, Yvonne Naef, Stephanie Blythe, Marcello Giordano, and Peter Serkin. Now Senior Lecturer in Voice at Iowa State University and recent recipient of the ISU Early Achievement in Teaching Award, Ms. Goble collaborates regularly in recital with bass-baritone Simon Estes and is the pianist and artistic director for the Simon Estes Young Artist Concert Series. She is the official pianist of the Metropolitan Opera Guild Auditions in Iowa and recitals regularly with artists affiliated with Des Moines Metro Opera; recent collaborators include tenor Taylor Stayton, baritone Michael Mayes, and sopranos Sarah Jane McMahon and Sydney Mansacola.

Ms. Goble holds bachelor's degrees in violin and piano performance from Olivet Nazarene University and a M.M. in collaborative piano and chamber music from Ball State University.

Ricky Ian Gordon (ASCAP)

b. 1956

www.rickyiangordon.com

Ricky Ian Gordon (b. 1956 in Oceanside, NY) studied piano, composition and acting, at Carnegie Mellon University. After moving to New York City, he quickly emerged as a leading writer of vocal music that spans art song, opera, and musical theater. Mr. Gordon's songs have been performed and or recorded by such internationally renowned singers as Renee Fleming, Dawn Upshaw, Nathan Gunn, Judy Collins, Kelli O'Hara, Audra MacDonald, Kristin Chenoweth, Nicole Cabell, the late Lorraine Hunt Lieberson, Frederica Von Stade, Andrea Marcovicci, Harolyn Blackwell, and Betty Buckley, among many others.

A highly prolific composer, Ricky Ian Gordon's catalog includes *Morning Star,* about Jewish immigrants in New York's Lower East Side in the beginning of the 20th century; *27,* about Gertrude Stein's salons at 27 rue de Fleurus; *A Coffin In Egypt*, a haunting tale of memory and murder, racism and recrimination; *Rappahannock County,* inspired by diaries, letters, and personal accounts from the 1860s; *Sycamore Trees*, a musical about suburban secrets and family; *The Grapes of Wrath*; *Green Sneakers*, a theatrical song cycle for Baritone, String Quartet, and Empty Chair; *Orpheus and Euridice*; *My Life with Albertine*; *Night Flight To San Francisco* and *Antarctica* from Tony Kushner's *Angels In America*; *Dream True*; *States Of Independence*; *The Tibetan Book of the Dead*; and *Only Heaven.*

Among his honors are an OBIE Award, the 2003 Alumni Merit Award for exceptional achievement and leadership from Carnegie-Mellon University, A Shen Family Foundation Award, the Stephen Sondheim Award, The Gilman and Gonzalez-Falla Theater Foundation Award, The Constance Klinsky Award, The National Endowment of the Arts, The American Music Center, and many awards from ASCAP, of which he is a member.

Mr. Gordon's works are published by Williamson Music, Carl Fischer Music, and Theodore Presser Company and available everywhere.

Cara Haxo (ASCAP)

b. 1991

chaxo91@gmail.com
www.chaxomusic.com

As a child, Cara Haxo (b. 1991) loved listening to stories read out loud. Today, she incorporates these stories, poetry, and artwork into her music. Haxo was awarded the 2013 National Federation of Music Clubs Young Composers Award, the 2013 International Alliance for Women in Music Ellen Taaffe Zwilich Prize, and second prize in the 2012 Ohio Federation of Music Clubs Student/Collegiate Composers Contest. She has been commissioned by the International Contemporary Ensemble, Quince Contemporary Vocal Ensemble, Splinter Reeds, and the PRISM Quartet, amongst other ensembles.

A native of Massachusetts, Haxo earned her Bachelors of Music in Composition at The College of Wooster, where she studied with Jack Gallagher and Peter Mowrey, and her Masters of Music in Composition at Butler University, where she studied with Michael Schelle and Frank Felice. Before Wooster, Haxo spent six summers studying at The Walden School Young Musicians Program in New Hampshire, where she has returned as faculty in recent years, teaching classes in composition, theory, and graphic notation. An avid Francophile, Haxo studied film, literature, and archeology at The Institute for American Universities in Aix-en-Provence, France, during the summer of 2011. Haxo is a doctoral candidate in composition at the University of Oregon, where she studies with Robert Kyr and David Crumb and works as a Graduate Teaching Fellow in Music Theory.

Cameron Lam (APRA AMCOS)

b. 1989

cameron.lam.cl@gmail.com
www.cameronlam.com

Cameron Lam is a freelance composer, the Artistic Director of Kammerklang, - Sydney-based hybrid-art production company - and the Art Music Specialist at APRA AMCOS.

His compositional experience has always been based in practical work and experimentation. An avid dabbler and appreciator of various artforms, he completed his honours in Composition at the Sydney Conservatorium of Music and studied dance and static trapeze for 7 years at B&B Studios in Marrickville.

In particular Cameron's approach to composition is inspired by game designer, Mark Rosewater and American theatre director, Anne Bogart. Both advocate the role and experience of the player in artistic expression, leading him to create pieces with more interaction and agency for the performer.

Cameron has had the pleasure of working with and writing for many of Australia's leading musicians such as acclaimed percussionist Claire Edwardes, vocal ensemble Halcyon, the Nexas Saxophone Quartet, clarinettist Sue Newsome, and YouTuber and EWI-ist Peter Smith.

Many of Cameron's works utilise narrative and myth in order to create structure. This element of myth infuses notable works such as Australia's first EWI (Electronic Wind Instrument) concerto, Electric Phoenix (Strathfield Symphony Orchestra) and the first contrabass clarinet concerto with wind symphony, Yggdrasil: The World Tree (Sydney Conservatorium Wind Symphony).

Cameron is proud to be an Australian Music Centre represented composer and Fine Music 102.5FM's 2018 Stephen Kruger Scholar. He is currently writing The Art of Disappearing, a song cycle for mezzo-soprano and string quartet, based on poetry by Australian author, Sarah Holland-Batt.

Cecilia Livingston (SOCAN)

b. 1984

cecilia.livingston@gmail.com
www.cecilialivingston.com

With music described as "haunting" and "eerily beautiful" (Tapestry Opera), British-Canadian composer Cecilia Livingston specializes in music for voice. She is a Social Sciences and Humanities Research Council of Canada Postdoctoral Fellow in Music at King's College London, and for 2019-2021 she will be embedded at Glyndebourne through their "Balancing the Score" emerging composer development program. She was a 2015-2017 Composition Fellow at American Opera Projects in New York. Her music has been performed by the Toronto Symphony Orchestra, at Nuit Blanche, and at Bang on a Can's summer festival. Winner of the Canadian Music Centre's 2018 Toronto Emerging Composer Award and the Mécénat Musica Prix 3 Femmes for female opera creators, she is working on Terror & Erebus, a chamber opera for TorQ Percussion Quartet and Opera 5. She has published in The Opera Quarterly, Cambridge Opera Journal, and Tempo, and has presented papers on contemporary opera at the Royal Musical Association and American Musicological Society annual conferences.

An associate composer of the Canadian Music Centre and a National Councilor of the Canadian League of Composers, her creative and research work is supported by the Canada Council for the Arts, the Ontario Arts Council, the Toronto Arts Council, the SOCAN Foundation, and the Social Sciences and Humanities Research Council of Canada. She holds a doctorate in Composition from the University of Toronto, where she was awarded the Theodoros Mirkopoulos Fellowship in Composition.

Twitter: @CeciliaComposer

Shona Mackay

www.shonamackay.com

Shona Mackay is a Glasgow-based composer whose work often includes a strong audiovisual element. With a keen interest in pushing the boundaries of what it means to be "the composer", particularly in relation to the idea of the non-musical performer, she combines music with other media including film, photography, spoken word and/or theatre. She often performs in her own works.

In 2016/2017 she worked with the Glasgow School of Art Choir as part of Making Music's Adopt a Composer scheme, in partnership with Sound and Music, BBC Radio 3 and PRS for Music Foundation. "Continuum", written specially for the choir, was performed in Kelvingrove Art Gallery and Museum, Glasgow in May 2017. Excerpts of the work can be heard in this BBC Radio 3 interview broadcast in early 2018.

Alongside composition, Shona works as an educator, facilitator and teaching artist in numerous arts and education projects across the West of Scotland, focusing on widening participation and embedding creativity into the curriculum.

Tony Manfredonia (BMI)

b. 1992

contact@manfredoniamusic.com
www.manfredoniamusic.com

With performances and readings from renowned ensembles such as Apollo Chamber Players, the University of Cambridge Concert Band in England, and the Pittsburgh Symphony Orchestra, Tony's music has been played internationally and is now published through both MusicSpoke and NewMusicShelf. Actively bringing new music to his Northern Michigan home, *Love Awakens: for concert band* was commissioned by the Mackinac Arts Council and premiered by the Straits Area Concert Band, celebrating Henry David Thoreau's bicentennial birthday. The same year, Tony made his way to Symphony Number One's Fourth Call for Scores as a semi-finalist. Other recent awards include Brazosport Symphony Orchestra's Composer Competition, the inaugural Texas A&M University's Composition Competition and Symposium, and a Merit Award in the Tribeca New Music Young Composer Competition.

He also lives the life of a video game composer, creating sonic spaces and emotionally-driven tracks to enliven each game's world. Recent and in-development soundtracks include *Kharon's Crypt* and *Call of Saregnar*. Continually branching out into various styles, two of his 2017/18 projects involved sacred music: the full, orchestral score for Saint Luke Productions' latest drama, *Tolton: From Slave to Priest*, and a Concert Band piece commissioned by Holy Ghost Preparatory School in Bensalem PA, *Rejoice in the Holy Spirit*, for a performance in September 2018.

Born and raised near Philadelphia, PA, Tony graduated from Temple University with a degree in Music Composition. During his time in college, he had the blessing of meeting Maria - a young equestrian from Northern Michigan - via his blog dedicated to mental health awareness. Ever since that sparked their marriage, he continually advocates those who suffer from mental illness. As an example, his latest opera, *Ghost Variations* — commissioned by OperaRox Productions — depicts the hardship Clara Schumann endured while her spouse, Robert, suffered through severe psychological sickness.

Twitter: @amanfr01
Instagram: @amanfr01
Soundcloud: https://soundcloud.com/tony-manfredonia
Facebook: https://www.facebook.com/tony.manfredonia

Nicole Murphy (APRA)

b. 1983

nicole@nicolemurphy.com.au
www.nicolemurphy.com.au

Nicole Murphy's music has been described as "exquisite and sensitive" (*Sydney Morning Herald*), "strong and compelling" (*Loudmouth*), and "full of exhilarating tension" (*Arts Knoxville*). She has been commissioned by eminent arts organisations including the Australian Ballet, the Royal Academy of Dance (London), the Melbourne Symphony Orchestra, Experiments in Opera/Symphony Space (New York), Orchestra Victoria, Wild Rumpus (San Francisco), Chamber Sounds (Singapore), and the Definiens Project (Los Angeles). Her music has been performed by the Tasmanian Symphony Orchestra, NOWensemble (New York), Ars Nova (Dallas), and Halcyon (Sydney), and has been programmed at numerous festivals, including the Norfolk/Yale Chamber Music Festival (Connecticut), the Dallas Festival of Modern Music, the Nief Norf Festival (Tennessee), the Atlantic Music Festival (Maine), and the Bowdoin International Music Festival (Maine).

Nicole is the recipient of various awards, including the inaugural Australia Ensemble Fellowship (2018), the ICEBERG International Call for Scores (2017), Nief Norf International Call for Scores (2016), the MAFB International Commissioning Prize (2015), the Theodore Front International Orchestral Prize (2013), and the Definiens C3 International Composer's Award (2011). She was chosen as the young composer to represent Australia at the 30th Asian Composers League Festival in Tel Aviv (2012).

Nicole holds a PhD from the University of Queensland and she is represented by the Australian Music Centre.

Twitter: @nicolejmurphy

Eric Pazdziora (ASCAP)

b. 1981

www.ericpazdziora.com

Eric Paździora is a composer whose music has been performed and published around the world. Reviewers have described his compositions as "fresh, exciting, and well-crafted" (*Pastoral Music*) and "an instant classic" (*Global Christian Worship*).

He holds a doctorate in composition from the University of Maryland, where he studied with of Mark Edwards Wilson. He was also a student of Mark Engebretson, Alejandro Rutty, and Edwin T. Childs. Additionally, he is a graduate of the European American Musical Alliance summer composition program in Paris, studying with pupils of Nadia Boulanger.

His D.M.A. dissertation, a one-act Scots-language chamber opera entitled *House of Winter*, tells the story of a woman's struggle with dementia. Other compositions similarly examine the balance between ancient traditions and contemporary concerns. The choral cycle *Canticles for the Holy Innocents*, composed in memory of child abuse victim Lydia Schatz, was premiered by Chorosynthesis Singers for their "Empowering Silenced Voices" concert series. Eric has also collaborated on several song cycles with award-winning author Jane Yolen.

In addition to his composing, Eric serves as organist and pianist at Epworth UMC in Gaithersburg, MD, and teaches at Chevy Chase School of Music.

Frances Pollock (ASCAP)

b. 1989

francespollockmusic@gmail.com
www.francespollock.com

Known for her "bold and bracing" (*Baltimore Sun*) opera writing, Frances Pollock's music "pulls no punches and never flinches." (*City Paper*)

Originally from North Carolina, Frances's music has been performed all over the country by the Bridge Ensemble, Prima Volta, The North Carolina Governors' School, Divine Waters Ensemble, and many others.

In 2015, she wrote her first opera, *Stinney*, which won multiple awards including John Hopkins University's Diversity Innovation Grant and Best of Baltimore award. From 2016-2017, Frances was composer in residence for the Divine Water's Ensemble. In 2016, Frances was commissioned by Washington National Opera to write a one-act opera entitled *What Gets Kept*.

Frances is a founding member of the new music non-profit, Prima Volta. She is a composition fellow with American Opera Projects and with the Aspen Summer festival.

Frances holds a B.M. in Theory and Composition from Furman University and a M.M. in Voice from Peabody Conservatory. She is continuing her graduate composition studies at Yale University.

Twitter: @francespollockcomposer

Julia Seeholzer (ASCAP)

b. 1990

www.juliaseeholzer.com

Julia Seeholzer's music has been described as "ingenious", "lyrical", and "gently offbeat." She is the recipient of multiple awards, including the American Prize for Composition (student choral composition, 3rd place, 2015) and the Laurie Anderson Women in Technology award. Julia's pieces have been played by many established groups, including the Esterhazy String Quartet, Urban Playground Chamber Orchestra, Trio D'esprit, and members of the Los Angeles Philharmonic. In 2011, she attended Yale University's New Music Workshop as a composition fellow to study with Martin Bresnick. Julia's work has been commissioned by the University of Chicago's Camerata, the Tenuto Chamber Singers, WomenSing, and others.

Julia recently completed her Master's degree in composition at the University of Cincinnati's College-Conservatory of Music, where she studied with Joel Hoffman. She takes much of her compositional influence from color – intervalic relationships conjure specific hues, which in turn dictate a piece's direction. When composing for voice, text further impacts each piece's color spectrum. Julia received her B.M. in composition from the Berklee College of Music, where she graduated summa cum laude; her principal teacher at Berklee was Marti Epstein.

Julia currently studies advanced choral writing with Paweł Łukaszewski in Warsaw, Poland, under a Fulbright research grant. Her project involves writing pieces for performance by Dr. Łukaszewski's choir, Musica Sacra.

Outside of composition, Julia is heavily involved in the world of video game music. In 2009, she founded the Video Game Music Choir (now PXL8) – an internationally recognized chamber choir that performs video game scores arranged exclusively by and for the group; she directed the group until 2012. Julia is constantly working on arrangements and collaborations, and has worked with the Videri String Quartet, as well as contributed to both the Harmony of Heroes and Spectrum of Mana projects.

Alan Theisen (ASCAP)

b. 1981

www.alantheisen.com

Alan Theisen is a composer, saxophonist, music theorist, and educator.

Theisen's compositions encompass a wide array of genres and instrumentation including chamber music, art song, solo piano, jazz, concerti, and more. Praised by composer Dimitri Terzakis as being "the product of a unique talent," his works are frequently commissioned by professional chamber musicians and large ensembles alike. Though Theisen's pieces are stylistically diverse, all exhibit unabashed emotional sincerity, memorable melodies, sensitive harmony, and carefully constructed formal designs—characteristics that inspire enthusiastic audience response and repeat performances. Some recent premieres of Theisen's music have occurred at National Sawdust (Brooklyn), New Music Gathering (Peabody Conservatory), and the World Saxophone Congress (Strasbourg, France).

An active saxophonist, Theisen concertizes in classical recitals, performs with jazz bands and musical theater productions, and premieres/records the music of fellow contemporary composers. His voice/saxophone duo, Megan Ihnen and Alan Theisen present..., performs curated programs of contemporary music across the United States to audience acclaim. To extend his mission as a collaborative performer, he founded and directs two larger ensembles: the Resonance Saxophone Orchestra and the Asheville Modern Big Band.

Theisen is associate professor of music at Mars Hill University where he has coordinated the music theory/composition curriculum since 2011.

Dennis Tobenski (ASCAP)

b. 1982

dennis@dennistobenski.com
www.dennistobenski.com

Dennis Tobenski is a composer of acoustic new music, a vocalist, and a strong advocate for new music and the interests of living composers.

Dennis' *Only Air*, a 20-minute work for high voice and orchestra memorializing the gay teenagers who have taken their own lives in recent years, was commissioned by the Illinois State University Symphony Orchestra, and has been performed in a chamber version by The Secret Opera in New York and members of the Bay Area Rainbow Symphony in San Francisco.

The voice features prominently in his catalog of works, with a special emphasis on working with texts by living poets. He has collaborated with such poets as Jorn Ake, Idris Anderson, Kathryn Levy, Elizabeth Seydel Morgan, Maggie Smith, Mark Statman, and Patricia Valdata.

Dennis received his B.Mus. in Vocal Performance and Music Theory & Composition from Illinois State University, and his M.A. in Music Composition from The City College of New York.

His principal teachers have included David Del Tredici, Chester Biscardi, Serra Hwang, Stephen Andrew Taylor, and David Feurzeig. He is a member of the Board of Advisors for Composers Now, and the Board of Directors of Perfect Enemy Records and KeyedUp MusicProject.

Dennis lives in New York City with his husband Darien Scott Shulman and their cat Pistachio.

Facebook: www.facebook.com/dennistobenski
Twitter: @dennistobenski

Moe Touizrar (SOCAN)

b. 1975

mtouizrar@gmail.com
https://soundcloud.com/moe-touizrar

Moe Touizrar is a composer, researcher, and concert organizer, whose artistic and theoretical interests converge on two broad areas — the perception of timbre and the study of musical meaning. Currently based between Montreal and Helsinki, his music has been performed in Canada, Europe, and the USA by ensembles such as the Total Cello Ensemble, Nouvel Ensemble Moderne, and Ensemble Transmission. He has participated in many festivals, including the Orford Summer Music Academy, Scotia Festival of Music, Rencontres de Musique Nouvelle at Domaine Forget, and in 2018 was selected composer-in-residence for the Kesä Virrat Soi festival in Finland. In 2016 he won the inaugural Andrew Svoboda Memorial Prize in Orchestral Composition. Moe Touizrar has been invited to present lectures on timbre and musical meaning at the Swiss Centre for Affective Sciences, the University of Jyväskylä, the University of Helsinki, and at the XIVth Congress of Musical Signification, in Cluj-Napoca, Romania. Moe Touizrar is currently a Ph.D. candidate in Composition and Music Perception at the Schulich School of Music, McGill University under the co-supervision of composer John Rea and experimental psychologist Stephen McAdams.

Ed Windels (ASCAP)

b. 1967

edwindels@gmail.com
www.ed-windels.com

The compositions of Ed Windels have been described variously as "nice, a little too long" (his aunt), "lacking a distinctive voice" (a renowned orchestral executive), "awfully repetitive with not much going on" (a highly regarded flautist) and "really really hard" (several performers, especially singers).

The first known (or at least acknowledged) member of either side of his family to display any artistic inclination, Ed squandered his youth in dilettante explorations of most of the fine and performing arts, before dismaying his parents by devoting his studies to the most unreliable and ephemeral, classical music, earning both Bachelors and Masters degrees in composition at the Mannes College of Music in just three years. Possessing little to no ability as a performer of any kind and a sanguine attitude about the challenges of making a full time living as a composer, he has earned his keep in the corporate world and as a "5 to 9" artist, a path he for which he has become an advocate. He has since developed a burgeoning side career as an arranger and orchestrator in theatrical world.

Ed has never earned a residency, won no awards or prizes, and holds no certificates or distinction of merit... yet. Outside of a showcase concerts of his works by NewMusicNewYork, his compositions have never received public recognition, although he has had the pleasure of being performed, albeit grudgingly, by some of New York City's most notable up-and-coming artists.

Supplementary Materials

Texts, program notes, composer biographies, and composer headshots can be found at:

https://newmusicshelf.com/anthologies/mezzo-v1-info/

www.ingramcontent.com/pod-product-compliance
Lightning Source LLC
Chambersburg PA
CBHW080341170426
43194CB00014B/2650